Collective Heart

A Compilation

KAZURI PRESS

Copyright © 2023 Mindie Kniss

All rights reserved. No portion of this book may be reproduced or utilized in any form or by any means, electronic or mechanical, including photocopying, recording, or by any information storage and retrieval system, without written permission from the publisher, except as permitted by U.S. copyright law.

Kniss, Mindie.

The collective heart: true stories of the invisible thread that connects us all / Mindie Kniss.

1. Heart intelligence

Cover image: bebuntoon

Paperback Edition ISBN-13: 978-0-9915055-2-4

eBook Edition ISBN-13: 978-0-9915055-3-1

Kazuri Press. An imprint of Lucra® LLC.

Published in the United States of America.

For Sean

The power of your heart still beats through all of our lives.

Contents

Epigraph	IX
Foreword	XI
1. Warm Hearts & Hot Toddies by Doug McDade	1
2. Can You Hear the Universe? by Elisha Ghorbani	9
3. Let This Not Be All There Is to My Life by Bettina Gordon-Wayne	17
4. Surviving Me by Steve Sconzert	27
5. Judgment or Compassion by Vauna Byrd	35
6. Holding Space by Lewis Denbaum	43
7. Finding My Wings by Carla Egurrola	51

8.	Ideas Are Indeed Worth Sharing by Bobby Kountz	59
9.	Follow the Resistance by Tiamo De Vettori	67
10.	The Inner Shitter by Sandra Rosenthal	75
11.	Feeding Families, Feeding Hearts by Jeremy Jackson	83
12.	Crash of Hearts by Jamie Del Fierro	91
13.	Don't Wait by Megan Love	99
14.	Lost by Josh Aronovitch	107
15.	Living a Rainbow Life by Vanya Slaveva	115
16.	Memorable by Jeremy Coombs	123
17.	Yes in Your Heart by Jeannette McGaha	127
18.	Plus One by Corinna Parish	135

19.	Angel in Red and Black Flannel by Patty Flock	141
20.	Uno by Mindie Kniss	149
21.	The Collective Heart by ChatGPT	159
Thank You for Reading		161
Also Available From Kazuri Press		163

"Connected to the collective heart, you can be certain in every cell of your being that you are never alone, and you will experience the grace, guidance and ease that comes when you are one with all there is."

~ Debbie Ford

Foreword

Dear Reader,

I have such gratitude to those who shared their personal stories in this book and to you, for your interest in reading them. My hope is that you will resonate with some of their experiences, or perhaps glean a new perspective through which to see the world.

There are infinite examples of the intricate connection points in life—far too many for mere coincidence. Just a few of them are documented herein.

So many thanks,
Mindie Kniss, MFA, PhD
Kazuri Press™/Lucra® LLC

P.S. You might smile at the reason I named my publishing imprint Kazuri...
When I took a small group to Kenya in 2017, we toured the Kazuri bead factory in Nairobi. One of my Kenyan friends

asked my husband, Sean, "Do you know what *Kazuri* means in Swahili?"

"What?"

"Small and beautiful."

Without skipping a beat, Sean beamed and said, "Oh, like me!"

Warm Hearts & Hot Toddies

by Doug McDade

In Memoriam: Karl "Tük" Wilson
July 22, 1952 – November 11, 2022

If this fire dies, we'll all freeze to death. This was my only thought as I stared into our makeshift firepit, a toolbox we had emptied out that was now filled with anything we could find that would burn in the back of our tour bus. My band and I were stuck in a snowstorm. We were cold and we were scared.

Murph, our lighting engineer, shoved a handful of empty Micky D's french fry sleeves in my face and some old song lists. "Here! Try these!"

I carefully fed the papers to the glittering, fading ashes. Mistin, our lanky Lennon-esque lead guitarist, was behind the wheel, with Tük in shotgun. They thumped their mittened hands in applause as they shivered and rocked, trying to keep warm.

"Can we get it going enough to burn Tük's drumsticks?"

Tük yelled back to us, "I'm not ready to give them up yet!"

Doc, our roadie and sound engineer, shouted back, "If we get out of here alive, I'll buy you a new set, dude!"

"If we get out of here alive…?" Yeah, "*IF.*" That's what we were all thinking.

Earlier that day, we had played a concert in Decorah, Iowa, and were en route to our next stop, Willmar, Minnesota. It was mid-February, so we expected about a four-and-a-half-hour trip. Traversing the Midwest's harsh winter elements meant our anticipated ETA was about 4:30 AM.

As we headed out, Tük was driving and Murph was riding shotgun. Mistin, Trion, our keyboardist, and I were sleeping in the back of the cab. It had been a weary tour, and Willmar was our final stop. We seemed to be making good time, so I was looking forward to some shut-eye before the sun came up.

As we rolled across the Iowa / Minnesota border, the snow was letting up, and the temperature was a balmy 40 degrees. The roads were clear, but as we approached

Minneapolis, it started to rain. It was coming down hard, and the road was slick. By the time we were north of the cities, the downpour had turned into a torrential freezing thunderstorm.

When we pulled into a truck stop in Minnetonka, everybody jumped out, relieved that the worst of our harrowing drive seemed to be behind us. Tük was a ball of nerves and asked if Mistin or Murph would take the wheel. Mistin agreed but wanted to get back on the road and to our hotel as soon as possible. The weather report on the radio was tracking a storm coming in fast from the west.

Back on the bus with our food in less than ten minutes, the gentle drizzle had turned into feathery snow flurries and the wind had picked up. By the time we hit Excelsior, the temperature had dropped twenty degrees. It was a full-scale blizzard thundering overhead, the lightning illuminating brief dismal images of the barren landscape being buried in snow. Visibility was barely a quarter mile ahead and we saw car after car spin out into the ditches.

Soon the landscape was littered with vehicles like skeletons in Death Valley. Mistin, ashen-faced and white-knuckling the steering wheel, was praying out loud that he could navigate the trenches and avoid the ones that led into the emptiness beyond the shoulder of the road. We were all paralyzed with fear. The snow was up to the axles, and if it continued, we'd be stranded for sure. I looked out at the cars that had pulled over. Some had their lights on and engines running. We couldn't stop to help them because we had to keep our momentum up. We were down to about thirty-five miles an hour. Suddenly, out of the stabbing white snow, a semi-truck flew right toward us and veered straight into a field to our right. We dodged a bullet. Then, we were down to twenty miles an hour and could feel our bus dragging bottom in the snow. We couldn't tell what side of the highway we were on. We jolted to a halt.

"That's it, boys," Mistin said. We were dead in a sea of arctic white. Our nearest neighbor was a half-buried car about fifty yards away. The cold, blizzard-force winds whistled through our bus while we idled for what seemed like hours, doing everything to keep the inside of the truck toasty warm. The snow was piling up, and soon, the tailpipes would be covered. We kept the windows open just a bit so as not to be overcome with poisonous gas. The snow drifted in through even the slightest crack of the windows. We had just gassed up about thirty miles back, but then, suddenly, the engine sputtered and stopped. We were out of gas.

No heat, stranded in the middle of a barren highway. How were we going to keep warm and not freeze to death?

So there I was, sitting in the back of the bus, freezing and fanning what was left of Tük's smoldering drumsticks, the lining of my guitar case, old magazines, fast-food wrappers, and playlists. The last spark faded into oblivion. It was now time for six guys to huddle together to preserve what heat we might still be generating. Freaked out and paranoid, with no sign of life visible through the ice on the windshield, I refused to close my eyes for fear I'd never wake up. If I was going to freeze to death, I would do it with my eyes open!

Suddenly, we heard an explosion off in the distance. And another one closer. Then a third right next to us, rocking the bus. The snow was an arctic squall, thunder and lightning crashing around us. Next to the bus, a roadside power pole streamed out arching flames and sparks. Murph surmised that the strain of the subversive cold was causing the transformers on the poles to explode. It felt like we were in a war zone and the world was ending.

All at once, I saw dozens of dancing lights like little orbs glistening through the frozen, frosted windshield. I shook Tük, asking him if he saw it too, or was I hallucinating on the brink of death? He sat up. Yelled to the others. No one seemed to know what we were seeing.

The lights split up. Some stopping while others bounced about in the snow. Without warning, three lights came charging straight at us! Trion was chanting religiously about how he believed in aliens. The next thing we knew, we were attacked by three roaring snowmobiles! One of the drivers jumped off his vehicle and banged on our window. "Anybody in there?" he shouted, barely audible over the howling winds.

"Oh my gosh! Yes! Yes, we are!"

The main door to the bus was frozen shut. The snow was too heavy to push it open from the inside, but somehow, the snowmobile operator was able to get it open. He climbed in with a brisk smile and explained in a husky voice that they were a snowmobile club from a neighboring town that decided to get together and search the highway for stranded travelers.

They had about thirty snowmobiles and these were the last four. We were in luck because each could carry two passengers. The next thing I knew, we were being whisked away into the abyss.

I was the only passenger on this motor sled and as we sped away, my pilot decided to head toward a stranded car about a hundred yards away. Inside was a lovely and vibrant 84-year-old lady who chortled that it was about time we arrived. She was tired of singing Tammy Wynette songs to herself. Covered in old shawls and blankets, she crawled onto our snow scooter. She got in between the driver and me. Once settled, she turned back to me with a big smile and exclaimed loud enough to shake the heavens, "I have always wanted to ride on one of these contraptions! Giddy-up, Cowboy! I love you guys! I really do. Let's hit the Iditarod!" And off we went - her arms waving in the frigid air, cackling like a happy hen. Granny was having the time of her life.

The snowmobilers delivered us to a little tavern in St. Bonifacius where we spent the next five days stranded. I was deeply grateful that a group of arctic-clad ski-chariot riders had such warm hearts to search for those lost in the wasteland. And that Granny was safe and able to share her love for mother nature, as well as being a pretty gosh darn good bartender. She smiled and shook her head and toasted her first-ever snowmobile ride. "When the weather gets cold, warm hearts and hot toddies are nuthin' but gold!"

Doug McDade is an award-winning Actor/Director/Film Maker, Musician, Song Writer, Recording Artist,

Entrepreneur, Speaker, and Master Coach. He is the Founder of the DOUG MCDADE STUDIO OF THE PERFORMING HeARTS™. He's performed with notable musicians, celebrated actors, and accomplished writers/directors like David Mamet and Abbey Mann. He was awarded the 2006 Volunteer of The Year Award from NorthPointe Resources of Zion, IL for creating an acting program with the developmentally disabled. Learn more at dougmcdadestudio.com or follow on Insta @dougmcdade.

Can You Hear the Universe?

by Elisha Ghorbani

Entrepreneurship can be lonely. You just put your head down and work. I knew I needed to do something, but I couldn't have expected what the Universe gave me.

I Googled "groups for entrepreneurs," and Genius Network® came up. I was coming out of the worst time of my life, where I felt like I was past the trauma but not past the effects of trauma.

Years earlier, I lost my family to lies and deceit. I was accused of being a monster. Was it true? No. Did it take three years of hell and hundreds of thousands of dollars to clean it up? Yes.

I eventually got my family back, but it was very different from what I'd expected. Just because you get your reputation back, just because you get your name cleared, just because everything is "fine" now doesn't make up for the intense trauma, pain, and hatred you built up over the years.

What was killing me was my hate for someone whom I viewed as the person who put me in that situation. I signed up for Genius Network to spark a shift in my life.

Before, I was happy, loving, and kind—also, naïve AF. I'd do anything for anyone. Through the nightmare I experienced with my ex, I developed into a man-hater. I didn't trust them and had a lot of walls built up toward them.

I felt like I had completely lost myself. I hated so much. So I was trying to find ways to distract myself, to give myself something to get involved in that was bigger than me and maybe would help me out of my current situation.

Business was what I did to survive. That's how I kept myself from killing myself.

There was a point where there was so much pain. I remember lying outside on my high-rise patio, surrounded by luxury and the life I'd created. And all I could think was, *I'm just going to die. I'm just so tired.* I wasn't spastic or bawling my eyes out; I just felt done.

That's when I started looking for things to keep myself busy and found Genius Network.

At my first meeting, I was skeptical, wondering if I had

wasted my money. When this little guy in a wheelchair rolled on stage, I thought, *Who is this little fucker?*

Within a few minutes, I knew that I needed to connect with him. He had something I needed, although I wasn't sure what that was.

Someone at my table mentioned that Sean Stephenson was amazing, but it was really expensive to work with him. That seed was all I needed.

After the event, I reached out to Sean, met him over Zoom, and set up a Breakthrough experience with him. From the moment we started talking online, I felt like he "saw" me. And a Breakthrough was right up my alley, one and done because I didn't have time for any more shit.

I thought if this didn't work, then I would kill myself, but I just needed to try so that I would know that I hadn't given up too early.

When I showed up in Scottsdale and met Sean and Mindie for dinner, I thought, *What the fuck am I doing here?* At that time, the pain was so intense that I was exhausted with life, but those two had such a different perspective and way of living life.

The night before, I almost canceled. I did not want to go through all my trauma again. I had gone to plenty of counselors over the years of pain, but the poison was always still there. The thorns hadn't been removed. So I decided to just stick with the plan.

The whole experience was so chill that I wondered, *Is this actually doing anything?* And then, there was an exercise where Sean made me write out why I hated my ex on a giant whiteboard. (I've had to do this same exercise many times since.) It was the biggest gift that he could have given me—it helped me see that I wasn't crazy and that I had to keep forgiving. It's easy to see the negative; it takes work to look for the positive, but that's what I needed to do. That's what started to change things for me.

I realize now that hate was eating me alive from the inside out. I was a shell of the happy, loving, kind person I used to be.

After the Breakthrough, I would text Sean whenever I was angry. I would be so mad, and Sean would be so sweet, reminding me to use the tools and forgive again. I appreciated the reminders because my anger would distract me from the path back to peace. I couldn't even give myself the grace to connect back to goodness.

The most significant gift that Sean and Mindie gave me was the ability to connect to God/Universe again. Whatever you want to call it.

When all the stuff happened with my ex, the way I viewed the world crashed. I was just like, Fuck you. Fuck

God. Fuck all those lies and bullshit that I got told and manipulated and brainwashed with. All there is is today. And that's a dangerous way to live. There's no joy. It's all just hard work.

What Mindie and Sean revived in me was that there is magic. There's something greater than us. There's connection. And love! That gave me the ability to redefine my spirituality. I could be a spiritual person without being religious.

I was like a tricycle that was broken. My brain was good. I was crushing it with work. My physical body was good. But I wasn't good spiritually.

When I did HeartPath® with Mindie, she expanded on what Sean had taught me. She was able to weave the Magic and Logic together. Sean very much helped with the feels and the processing, and then Mindie was able to step in with the rationale and get my intellect involved. She showed me how these things DO work together. The Universe and the magic are logical; you just have to be open minded enough to see the connections. Sean got me to a point, then Mindie opened up another whole world for me to explore and learn about.

When Sean died, I felt so selfish because, yes, I was sad about my mentor and friend, but I also felt like someone had taken my training wheels away.

This thought kept Sean alive for me: *Elisha, what do you think I would say if I were talking to you right now?*

"I've completely fucked up."

No, I have faith in you that you got this. And you still have people there to support you.

I had Mindie. I wanted to love her at that moment for everything she had lost and for her to know how much I cared for her, but there was also the other side of me like, "Mindie, hey, whenever you're better, I do want to talk to you about me getting through the rest of this shit." I knew she was so strong. Mindie was the strong and quiet; Sean was the strong and loud.

There was a lot of discovery in this process, like learning how to forgive, learning how to re-forgive, learning how to work through all those things. They opened the door for me and ignited the flame that I myself had put out.

I got to the point where I could think, *Elisha, you're pretty fucking awesome.* And not awesome because you can make money. Those things are awesome, yes, but that's not the real cool shit. The real cool shit is, Can you hear the Universe? Can you step out of your own way and be connected to goodness?

When I meditate now, I say, "Please show me where I'm

getting in my own way." I know that the connection is there for all of us. We don't have to try to be worthy, but you're only going to receive what you think you're worthy of receiving.

The Universe would have gotten me here if I hadn't met them, but Sean and Mindie were a fast track. Whenever I allow myself to trust in that love and connection, crazy awesome shit happens. I'm just trying to stay out of my own way here.

Trust and love. That's it. If you ask for it, you'll get it.

Elisha is known for her real-life lessons and anecdotes from motherhood, entrepreneurship, relationships, self-love, and discovery.

She built a portfolio of companies spanning industries from food service to construction to real estate development. These include two companies at 8-figure revenue and seven companies at 7-figure revenue.

Elisha's key entrepreneurial skill is her ability to build SOPs. She has brought her game-changing insights to hundreds of organizations. To learn more, follow Elisha on Insta @ElishaGhorbani.

Let This Not Be All There Is to My Life

by Bettina Gordon-Wayne

I woke up in a panic. Unexpected. Sharp. Seemingly out of nowhere.

I glanced over at my husband sleeping next to me, his breathing relaxed and rhythmic. My eyes scanned the room with its familiar furniture, our travel pictures on the walls, yesterday's clothes flung over the back of the chair, and the drawn curtains barely hiding the morning glow. It was quiet on the street. Peaceful. The weekend.

We were in our house in Washington, DC, a mere stone's throw away from the world-famous Capitol building.

As I lay there, surprised by the sudden wave of sheer terror, involuntarily holding my breath, I felt a pain in my gut that drove tears to my eyes. I wasn't able to hide my agony any longer.

With deep anguish, I said to myself: "Dear God, let this

not be all there is to my life. There MUST be more than this... Right?!"

I was 42 years old, and I was terrified that I had missed my chances at the life I dreamt about two decades earlier.

The high-flying dreams of my youth had often crashed like the kites I flew as a child. By now, I had amassed a small army of disappointments which, like all good soldiers, marched up and down in my head with great discipline and vigor.

All the thoughts I ever had of being a colossal failure - of not being good enough, of giving my best and still not succeeding - came rushing back that morning. And with every marching soldier of defeat came the realization that I would have to bury more dreams soon because, at my age, the window of opportunity was closing fast.

. Soon it would be too late.

You know what I am talking about, don't you?

The feeling of "it's getting too late," or "I'm getting too old," or "I should have..." can creep up like love handles and muffin tops - stealthy and steady. It felt like there was a lot to be anxious about: What new career should I embark on at my age? Do I still want to have a child or was it too late? Write a book? Create financial abundance?

Had I missed the opportunity to follow my desires? Because, *realistically*, if I hadn't succeeded yet, what were the odds of achieving it later?

That morning on Capitol Hill, I fell headfirst into victimhood and martyrdom. I could *not* see all the dreams I'd already made come true. Instead, I sunk deep into the conventional thinking that my life would only become duller, more physically challenging, and less desirable with every passing year.

Then, out of nowhere, I had a flashback. I remembered standing in the high desert of the American West, listening to a revered elder from an ancient culture who opened my heart and gave me a formidable yet slithery gift - the gift of the snake.

It was right after a desert storm had died down. We could smell the scent of sage, sweetgrass, and wet soil, the distinctive scent of the red New Mexican earth after a downpour. Mother Nature was quiet now, and we sat in a circle in the grass. Then, suddenly, I was startled by a scary rustling behind me in the bushes. I jumped up with a yell.

"What is it?" said Oh Shinnah.

"I don't know, but it could be a snake!"

"So?"

"So? There are rattlesnakes here! You know that, right?"

The group laughed. Of course she did; this was her land. We had all come to be with this wise woman with her long white hair in braids. Two braids flowed down over her shoulders. The third one, though, on the side of her head, decorated with a red-tailed hawk feather, was more than a convenient hairstyle. This third braid signified her status as a Warrior Woman of the Apache People. It showed the world that she had gone through the ancient warrior training of her tribe, which, back then, was usually reserved for males only. The third braid told everyone they better not mess with her.

Oh Shinnah was zooming in on me. So I told her about how snakes plagued me in my dreams. How these slithery beasts frightened me and how I was disgusted by them. Oh Shinnah looked intensely at me and said, "Have you ever thought that snakes are your allies, your friends?"

"What do you mean?" I asked, thinking, *Hell, n-o-o-o.*

"Snakes are a symbol for rebirth and rejuvenation," she continued. "They shed their old skin, become anew. Since they come to you often in your dreams, they might be your most powerful allies."

"Ahhhhh...."

"Tomorrow, you should go up to the mesa and find a rattlesnake. Sit and communicate with it. The snake might have a message for you and your transformation."

Talk to a poisonous serpent? Was she crazy? Then I saw the third braid. "OooooKayyyy," I said.

Please backtrack with me for a minute: I was not your

usual snake whisperer. I was a business journalist who lived in Manhattan at that time. I usually charmed billionaires, not snakes. I believed in numbers, facts, and science and (wrongly) judged them superior to my instincts. To top it off, I grew up in Europe, thousands of miles away from any exposure to Native Americans and their traditional ways of living.

Yet, here I was because I had seen a flyer with Oh Shinnah's picture that ignited my adventurous soul. "Go on this journey," my inner daredevil demanded. I had immediately signed up for something - a spiritual journey others had prepared years to take - that I knew nothing about.

Now I was just minutes away from a mind-blowing authentic Native American ceremony, getting schooled in animal speak.

I once heard that when the student is ready, the teacher will appear. Mine showed up as a Native American Warrior Woman, seemingly from another world, yet intimately connected to me on a spiritual level. She recognized parts of herself in me. Oh Shinnah knew how to reach my heart and soul that were longing for adventures like "talking to rattlesnakes."

And, yes, I did go up to the mesa the next morning looking for chatty rattlesnakes. I found none, which may have saved me a hospital trip.

As it turned out, I only needed a radical shift in perspective - completely outside of societal norms and conventions - to transform anyway. I needed to honor the adventurer I was born to be: the inner Wild Woman I found in the Wild West. Oh Shinnah saved me years of therapy.

I discovered that my inner guidance, my dreams, and my Wild - the untamed part in all of us that we need to live into to find true happiness and peace - were there to guide and protect me, even if they looked dang scary at first.

What if my fears of a life not fully lived and years passing by were once again the snakes reminding me to shed my old skin and become anew? That morning in DC, I let my Wild take over and transform my midlife crisis into the most exciting decade of my life so far:

I embarked on an intriguing new career; decided to have a baby and birthed my naturally conceived son at 44; wrote my first bestselling book, The Joy of Later Motherhood; and even embraced my breast cancer diagnosis as I had once embraced the serpents: with love. I had a deep knowing that I could turn my cancer from a foe into a teacher and eventually my "healing partner" that helped me finally heal old emotional wounds.

The older I get, the more rebellious and free I've become

because I learned to honor my nature: I'm happiest when exploring new places, new lifestyles, and new ways of thinking. My Wild, as I call it.

We all need to heed our Wild. Without it, you'll never be complete. Nor truly happy. Without it, you'll never know what you are capable of.

A writer-at-heart-and-soul needs to see words come alive even if no one else will see them. A singer needs to feel her vocal cords vibrate. A painter connects to her spirit with her brush. A farmer feels alive when running soil through his fingers. A healer needs to heal. And I need change and excitement to feel fully alive.

I was never afraid of getting older, but of falling victim to societal prejudices around age and the BS that we, especially women, become less desirable, less visible, and less important with age. Today I'm having the time of my life smashing stereotypes and rewriting the script for women in their 40s and 50s as I guide them to live their Wild and create extraordinary lives.

Your Wild, whatever it is, needs to become non-negotiable, especially now, after years of isolation, fear, and social distancing. Now is the time to forge ahead. Out of the ashes, a Phoenix is born. Can you hear her calling?

Last month, I drove my young son to Pennsylvania to

introduce him to the Amish people who, if they belong to the Old Order, still farm their land with horses and educate their children in one-room schools from 1st-8th grade. We were fascinated and enlivened to learn from them, taste their food, ride in their horse buggy, and explore their world as much as they would let us in.

On that trip, I took Hunter for archery lessons. I watched with joy as this boy touched his own wildness every time he picked up the bow and arrow. Then I drew the bow, bringing the string to the corner of my mouth. I slowly breathed out and let the arrow fly across the range with great force. I didn't care where the arrow landed, as I knew one thing for sure: today, my life is right on target.

Bettina Gordon-Wayne is a seasoned journalist, bestselling author, and certified mental strength trainer. She helps women in their 40s, 50s, and beyond get Younger With Age and find their "Wild." Join Bettina on "My Year of Getting Younger," during which she shares all she learns about turning back the clock for your body, mind, and spirit at BettinaGordon.com/heart or follow her on YouTube @GetYoungerWithBettinaGordon.

Surviving Me

by Steve Sconzert

It was early summer in 2014, and I was listening to a podcast by a well-known pickup guru. She mentioned this motivational speaker named Sean Stephenson as a role model for guys with disabilities who are looking to build confidence and connect with women. That was me. Still alone after a divorce three years earlier, I wasn't exactly brimming with confidence and bravado. The podcaster went on to talk about how Sean, while three feet tall and in a wheelchair, was a total badass with women.

I could not have cared less about the motivational speaking, but learning how he gets women—that, I wanted!

"Interesting," I said. "I'll have to check him out."

My research revealed that Sean was an accomplished speaker and a clinical hypnotherapist who did full-day breakthrough sessions to help clients release emotional baggage and gain confidence. The cost was a significant investment (and risk), but having been down the path of traditional therapy that frankly went nowhere, I was ready to rip the band-aid off and get through my crap.

After an email and Skype introduction, I spoke with Sean about coming to see him in Scottsdale, Arizona, for that breakthrough. During that meeting, I got my first taste of what it meant to exceed expectations, a concept I would repeatedly experience while working with Sean and his wife, Mindie, who also became one of my coaches.

Included with my breakthrough day were admission to $10K Speeches, his three-day public speaking event, and enrollment in his six-month professional speaker Master Class.

Exceed expectations, overdeliver, surprise and delight. Call it what you will; Sean and Mindie lived what it meant to be generous with your gifts. Through their example, I learned that utilizing my gifts to serve the world generously is at the core of *The Collective Heart*.

While still not interested in speaking, I was determined to get my money's worth and take the class. "Besides," I thought, "maybe I'll meet someone to hook up with."

At $10K Speeches, I was amazed at how Sean commanded the room. He led the audience on an emotional journey through interviews with industry heavyweights Larry Winget to Dean Graziosi, to heartfelt breakthroughs with audience members. It was no accident. Born with Osteogenesis Imperfecta (a.k.a. brittle bone disease), Sean's condition provided the adversity he used to build resilience and confidence. At some level, I understood. My spinal cord injury, sustained at 18 when I wrecked my Camaro after a late-night party, forced an abrupt adjustment to life in a wheelchair. But, while I, too, learned to channel adversity into success, I was nowhere close to Sean. Further, I had somehow lost my edge.

I wanted the edge back.

I wanted a life fulfilled.

I wanted a girlfriend!

Two days later, I showed up for my breakthrough, hopeful and still intimidated by this tiny powerhouse of a man.

"If there's anyone who can cut through my layers of BS, it's gotta be Sean."

I could not have been more wrong—consciously. When the breakthrough was over, my brain felt like scrambled eggs. I entered with an expectation that a new me would emerge by the end of the day. A confident, self-assured, better version of who I was. A new me appeared all right, but it was more like a chick breaking through its shell and seeing life for the first time. I was gangly, awkward, and shaky, but the transformation had begun. The re-wiring of my neurology was not a one-and-done deal. Instead, it was the beginning of a continuous process.

While I could not see it at the moment, a huge lesson was revealing itself: Fulfilling my wish was a process, not a destination. A goal is just an endpoint that births a new desire. If I don't enjoy the process of getting there, I'll always be chasing.

Then came Master Class, Sean's advanced speaker training course. I was not looking forward to it. Intuitively, I knew it would be good for me, but so was having my wisdom teeth removed. I was sure there would be pain and plenty of opportunity for embarrassment in front of the class.

Further, the course culminated with an in-person competition where each student gave a ten-minute presentation. The prize? $1,000 in cash and the opportunity to deliver the winning talk at the following $10K Speeches event. My goal had nothing to do with money or making a speech at his event. It was simply to survive and not embarrass myself.

I learned a ton about becoming an effective presenter through the next several months of group calls, video assignments, and dripped content. Surprisingly, I survived all of it, and I think I did pretty well at times.

As time drew near for the competition, I became more

nervous and unsure.

"What the hell am I going to teach? I don't have a message in me. Besides, this is not my thing."

One week before the road trip to Arizona and the competition, I had my final dress rehearsal call with Sean. I don't recall what I put together. I think it was akin to apologizing for being new and nervous as a speaker—not exactly compelling content that would move an audience.

Then I heard what I didn't want to hear, but needed the most: "Steve, you might get some polite applause for this, but if you want to do something worthwhile, you need to start over."

Snap. There was my breakthrough.

At the moment, it was crushing. It also lit in me a fire to live up to my capability. Sean knew I had it in me, and he refused to allow me to not live up to it. He believed in me before I did.

"Okay, time to get back to work."

I had one week to remake my speech, prepare and pack for this trip—with no time off from my job.

So I ditched the old sob story and pulled out the real message. The one that was in me the whole time and needed to get out. It was my survivor story. It was the world's survivor story. The one the world needed to hear again to love and heal itself.

I finished putting it together only two days before leaving for Arizona. I practiced for whoever was nearby to listen; my daughter, close friends, and my housekeeper (with a language barrier, I doubt she understood much). Finally, during the 18-hour drive across Texas, New Mexico, and Arizona, I traded my usual music playlists and audiobooks to practice my talk.

When the day came for the competition, I felt like I had a credible speech. I would not embarrass myself if I didn't forget what to say. That was my only goal—and my biggest fear.

The fear was unfounded. I surprised myself by how well I delivered my speech. Once I started talking, it was as if words were coming through me, not out of me. It felt incredible! Afterward, it was like a giant weight was lifted. Part of it, I'm sure, was relief that I didn't forget anything.

But it turned out to be much bigger and more lucrative than that. I won the competition!

That's right, Steve Sconzert, the guy who six months ago would rather have a bikini wax than be a speaker, won a speaking competition.

In the end, I'm not sure what would have happened had Sean not believed in me and pushed me to my capabilities. He could have played it safe and let me deliver a mediocre speech. His impact was far more than just one speech for one class. Sean made a stand for me. It was the breakthrough I needed to believe in myself.

I am forever grateful for Sean and Mindie's example of exceeding expectations, growth through the process, and the power of belief.

They embodied the essence of the Collective Heart.

Oh, and the girlfriend I wanted? In 2016, I met Carol, an incredible woman that came into my life during this journey. There is no doubt that without this transformation, she would never have "seen" me.

On September 16th, 2018, Carol and I were married. Sean presided over the ceremony.

How has not believing in yourself cost you? For Steve Sconzert, it nearly cost him his life. Now, through his own survivor story and journey to self-acceptance, Steve has a passion for guiding others to see their own self-worth and live empowered purpose-driven lives. To learn more and connect with Steve for coaching or to speak to your group, visit SteveSconzert.com.

Judgment or Compassion

by Vauna Byrd

The garage door whirs shut. My parents are back. I wait in my room, listening as my siblings trickle off to bed. Mom picked up Dad from the airport. He'll know by now. I told her to tell him so I don't have to. Once the house is quiet, I creep down the stairs with trepidation. How will Dad react to my pregnancy? My sixteenth birthday was only a few months ago.

Every Sunday since I was born, my parents would herd the entire family into church. It felt comfortable, routine, warm. It wasn't until we moved to a new area when I was 12 that I realized not everyone goes to church. I started to consider why I attended, and I realized that it came from feelings deep within, a personal connection to God, not something my parents made me do or from routine or tradition.

My family studied the scriptures together daily. This took a lot of coordinating, as I was the fourth of ten kids. We learned the commandments and every Christian virtue repeatedly and with clarity. Especially the law of chastity. This was the big one. I knew to respect myself and my body, and to dress and behave modestly—skirts and shorts to the knees, sleeves, no cleavage. There were recurrent lessons throughout my life about saving virtue for marriage.

At 15, I thought my boyfriend was the best. He knew I didn't drink or smoke, so he quit both for me. He respected me. He never pressured me to do anything I didn't want to do. At that point in our lives, I knew what I wanted out of life, and I was sure he did too. I wanted to be a wife and a full-time mom, love on my babies, and fill our home with warmth and love, just like my mom. What more was there?

Every day after school, I spent the afternoon at my boyfriend's house. Sometimes I felt like we should go to my house. But with all the kids, noise, and restrictions, we could more easily get to know each other at his house. I discovered that not all parents have the same rules. At his house, his parents didn't care if we spent all our time alone in his room. That would never happen at my house, but his parents seemed to expect it. We talked and talked. After a couple of months, we moved on to other things—first kissing, then touching. It happened so naturally, but I felt conflicted about it. Sometimes I cried when I got home because I felt dirty. Still, I went over there every day because I loved him so much, and I knew he loved me. And I couldn't seem to control the urge to be with him.

My parents were the epitome of what I think Christ would want his followers to be. I always felt loved, valued, and important. Except they didn't know how to have difficult conversations. I think He would want that in parents. When I was in sixth grade, Madonna's hit song "Like a Virgin" topped the charts. I asked my mom what a virgin was. She said, "A pure and virtuous woman." I didn't know it had anything to do with sex because I knew nothing of sex yet. I ended up learning about sex from kids my age. In 9th grade, one of my classmates asked if I gave good head. I had no idea what he was talking about but pretended and responded with, "Wouldn't you like to know?"

The first time we had sex, I left abruptly and ran home feeling paralyzed. I crumpled on the floor. My shoulders heaved; I couldn't hold back the sobs. Tears cascaded like Multnomah Falls, relentless, never ceasing. He was an addiction. Maybe my guilt was an addiction. Every day, we had sex. Every day, I ran home feeling filthy. Every night,

I writhed in emotional pain, caressing my anguish. I'd ensnared myself in a vicious loop that I could not escape. This continued for a few months until something in me changed. I felt...different. I sensed that I was pregnant. Then my period didn't come. I wasn't surprised. But I was in shock.

I creep down the stairs with trepidation. Dad's back is to me; he's putting dishes in the dishwasher. "Dad?" My voice squeaks in a hush. He turns, tears flowing down his cheeks. His gentle arms embrace me. He sobs on my shoulder, and I on his. Eventually, he composes himself enough to speak. "I can't imagine what you've been going through."

We've always been a church-going family. But how could I go to church when I was starting to show, and the word would spread like flood waters in the desert?

I tell a close friend, Linda, an older woman with kids my age. She's taken the time to connect with my sisters and me and loves us without judgment. She is kind, supportive, and loving. A few weeks go by. She pulls me aside in the hall at church, whispering in my ear, "Happy Mother's Day!" This is the first acknowledgment of my pregnancy on Mother's Day. I feel a flicker in my heart, the beginning of a feeling. A feeling that maybe I don't have to be ashamed.

I finish my tenth-grade year at Columbine High School. Only a few close friends know I'm pregnant. My boyfriend's parents rush us into marriage. No one asks me how I feel. And it seems like the right thing to do, so I ignore the feeling of unease stirring in my heart.

After the wedding, my bishop tells me I should attend classes with the women instead of the youth. No way! Those are my mom's friends, not mine. So from then on, every week after service, I leave instead of going to class. A couple of months slip by, and I feel in my heart that I want to be in class, even if it means going with all the old ladies.

If there's judgment from them, I am unaware, although maybe naïve. I'm surprised because I feel at home. I'm the youngest female in the group by far. Friendships form. Bonds grow. I have mentors, mothers of all ages and stages. I only feel love.

School starts again and I attend a school for teen moms. Three months into my junior year, my daughter is born. Who knew I could love a person with such depth of my soul? She's beautiful. She's perfect in every way. Then the crying starts. Sometimes I don't know how to soothe her. At times I sit, helpless, tears flowing because nothing seems to help. I haven't yet learned that it's ok to let a baby cry for a bit after doing everything I can. So it rips my heart open. But I see my mom often; she's always been the perfect motherly example. And at church, there are other moms with whom I'm developing friendships. I feel connected there, though I feel alone at home.

Linda hosts a baby shower. I'm surrounded by a large group of girls and women, friends my age and new friends with more life experience and wisdom. I feel accepted, held, loved.

When my baby is six weeks old, I return to the school for teen moms. I bring her with me. She stays in the nursery while I attend classes. They come for me when she is hungry, and I can nurse her during class. I mention my baby shower at school, and one of the other moms says, "What church do you go to? I wouldn't dare show up at church!"

It took me many years to formulate what my dad taught me the day he found out I was pregnant. He taught me that the person is always more important than the situation. I've worked to integrate this learning as a part of myself, and I practice it in my interactions with others, especially my own family.

I'm grateful for the support I received at a critical time in my life. Linda opened the door for the other ladies to learn to love when they might have condemned. Everybody should have a Linda in their life.

- How can you remember that the person is always more important than the situation?

- Who can you help to feel supported and loved?

- Is there someone who could use your understanding instead of your judgment?

If you replace judgment with compassion, you might change the trajectory of another person's life for the better, as Linda did for me.

Vauna Byrd is a family coach, speaker, and singer. She is passionate about helping struggling parents give their kids stability, like she learned to, through creating a solid marriage and greater joy in family. Vauna's first priority is her marriage and family. She and her husband Roland have been married 21 years and counting. She is a mother of 6, stepmom to 3, and currently grandmother to 6. Vauna is writing her first novel. Visit VaunaByrd.com or follow @vaunabyrd.familycoach.

Holding Space
by Lewis Denbaum

May 12, 1999
The outskirts of Fairfield, Iowa

There I was with my wife (let's call her Alice), my two children, and 20 of our closest friends. We stood in front of our newly constructed dream home. After a year and a half of busting our asses, we had completed the house and were ready to move in. We designed a move-in ritual. At the appointed time, we all marched around the house, chanting and shouting with joy, "Victory!" After three revolutions, we crossed the threshold, proceeded to the dining room, and stood in front of a scrumptious sheet cake. We lit a candle in the center of the cake and each of our friends, one by one, lit a candle offering a wish for our new life in our new home. We felt fulfilled.

That night my wife and I collapsed into our new

king-size bed. As I drifted off to sleep, I felt her hands exploring and caressing me. I was delightfully surprised. She had *never* before initiated intimacy. I thought I had died and gone to heaven.

We were happy in our new home. Alice started a diet and exercise routine. She was losing weight and becoming more chipper. She bought new clothing to adorn her new shape, making her look years younger. She washed the streaks of gray from her jet-black hair. Life was good! Then without notice, the tables turned.

My life changed dramatically overnight. It was like I went into a movie theater and started watching *Mary Poppins*, went out to get some popcorn, and came back to find myself in a different theater by mistake where they were showing Alfred Hitchcock's *Psycho*.

One of the major life changes was when our sacrosanct Saturday date night was no longer definite. One week in July, I asked my wife of 21 years, the mother of my two children, what she wanted to do on Saturday night. She said, "Oh, I'm going out with Mary and some other women."

Another change was when Alice decided to go camping on a particular weekend even though she had previously resisted family camping trips. When she went camping, she wouldn't call home to talk to me or our kids while she was gone. She was becoming remote, spending much of her time in her home office on her computer. Clearly, my wife had been invaded by some extraterrestrial life force that took away her wonderful and loving personality!

November 1999

I walked into Alice's home office the day before Thanksgiving to get a pen. I noticed an email on her computer that confirmed, to my horror, that my marriage was in trouble. I confronted her about the content of the email. "How dare you read my emails," she yelled.

I raised my voice and responded, "How dare you write an email like that!" And just like that, a thick wall of estrangement went up between us.

My life felt like it had fallen apart. My nerves were jangled. When I'd bump into my friends in town, I would spontaneously start crying. I was an emotional mess. Then some of my friends recommended I attend a men's weekend called The New Warrior Training Adventure. So on December 2, 1999, I went off to this weekend. After participating in some masterful exercises on this "retreat," I developed my mission statement: *"To create a world of connection by unconditionally loving myself and others."*

I returned from the New Warrior Training Adventure

with a new sense of purpose in my life. However, the stress of daily living with marital estrangement made me feel like a ball in a ping-pong match; my emotions went back and forth.

First, I'd say to myself, "Okay, I'm going make this marriage work." The next day I'd tell myself, "No, I can't keep going in this marriage." This went back and forth in a relentless manner for months.

My strength during this time was my men's group. It was comprised of men who were veterans of The New Warrior Training Adventure that I had just completed. We all shared the experience of that transformative process.

These men were there week in and week out to support me with my challenge. Every meeting would start with a "check-in," which is a report of the current status of one's life. My check-in was always the same: "I don't know if I can make this marriage work, but I want it to work. I've got two kids. I don't want to break up my family. But the estrangement is deep. I don't know what to do." Each week demonstrated that I was stuck in a negative emotional loop. I'd return to the men's circle every week with the same narrative, sounding like a broken record. The men must have found me unbearable, but they listened and held space for my check-ins.

July 2000

Months later at my men's group, I repeated my story. I concluded my check-in with the now-familiar sentence: "I don't know what to do."

The silence in the room was thick. Then, after what seemed like an eternity, Big Jim spoke up. His voice was loud, forceful, and firm. "Denbaum, we've been hearing this same pitiful story every week for months! What are you going to do?"

Wow, this stunned me! Big Jim's question seemed harsh, yet I knew it came from a place of love. He was right. My indecision had gone on long enough. It was time to take control of my life!

Then I said, "Let me think this through. If I stay in this marriage for the sake of our children, knowing what I know is going on, I'm not going to get any love from my spouse, so I have to learn to love myself. I'm going to have to be strong.

If I end the relationship, I'll be on my own. I'll still need another source of love. And I'll need to be strong." Then the light bulb went on! I said to the men in my group, "Ah, you know what? I don't have to make a choice between leaving or staying. No matter which path I take, I need to be strong and develop self-love. So I don't need to make a decision about my matrimonial state now; I can immediately start to develop self-love and inner strength. Then I'll be prepared for either eventuality. It was a beautiful moment. I felt relieved and empowered. I had the power to control my destiny. The solution wasn't about WHAT to do. It was about who I needed to BE.

I walked out of that meeting knowing I could follow my mission—to create a world of connection by loving myself and others, no matter how my marital conflict unfolded.

I'm grateful to each man in that group for his support over those six months, for holding space and listening without judging me. It finally hit me—my life is not loveless. I have men in my group who love me, and I love them.

That's not the end of the story. There is a postscript. Alice and I lived together for three more years in estrangement, in the same house filled with tension and no communication. We divorced in July 2003 and I entered that dangerous territory called "Dating after 50."

It was scary. I had to do things I hadn't done for 35 years, like asking a woman to go on a date with me. I'd pick up the phone, dial a woman's telephone number, and hang up before it rang. I said to myself, "Geez, this is what I used to do when I was in high school." I know I wanted a new intimate relationship and I knew I didn't want to fall into a rebound relationship. I had to discover what qualities in a woman matched mine. Again, my men's group supported me. They made sure that I loved and honored myself. That meant I dated many women, interacted with different feminine energies, and allowed myself to get to know ME. It was time for me to *"create a world of connection by unconditionally loving myself and others."*

Lewis Denbaum is a certified coach in dating, relationships, and transformation. He is a certified Jack Canfield Success Principles trainer. Lewis has been participating in and leading men's groups since 1994. He helps divorced men heal from anger, sadness, guilt and shame, and catapult themselves into a more empowered life. He has taught meditation since 1975 and offers it to his clients when appropriate. Earlier in his life, he practiced as a lawyer and CPA.

Finding My Wings
by Carla Egurrola

It was November 1, 2015, my 41st birthday. I was on the floor, curled up in the fetal position, silently screaming and crying my heart out. What had just happened can only be described as sheer madness between my husband and me. There were screams and punches; I even ripped our marriage photos.

A few weeks before this excruciating moment, I had made one of the most difficult decisions of my life: I gave up on a project where I had invested my inheritance, my savings, and more than five years of my time. It had taken me more than a year to muster the courage to leave the company I co-founded and risk the loss of all I had invested, which was, basically, everything I had.

I could never have imagined what was about to unfold. By making the decision to give up the company and be true to my heart and soul, the Universe led me to face an even greater challenge.

Shortly after my resignation, the avalanche came. I was getting ready to teach a yoga class when I received a call. I was not prepared for what happened next.

Fifteen minutes before class, I was on the phone with a woman who told me a soap opera-type story filled with betrayal, secrets, another relationship, and infidelity. I could feel my heart breaking into a thousand tiny pieces. Her words and the accompanying thoughts they created were crushing. My husband was cheating on me with a woman who was a yoga student at my studio, and apparently, it had been going on for two years.

As I hung up the phone, my shattered heart racing, I walked from my office, passed through the cafe on the way to the yoga studio, and found my husband waiting to come to class.

I glared at him as we silently walked into the studio. I was struggling to hold myself together. My heart kept pounding, and my head was spinning. I was awash in emotion, trying to center myself while directing "inhale, upward dog, exhale, downward dog…" Needless to say, I was far from present.

I suddenly realized that I wasn't just losing my business and giving up after five years of pouring myself into it. I was also looking at giving up my marriage of seven years with my five- and seven-year-old kids to support.

I would have to start my life over from scratch and leap toward... Well, whatever would come next. And I really had no idea what was coming.

Deep down, however, despite the pain and the chaos, I knew I would be ok, that I would come out stronger. I was ready to take that leap of faith for a new life.

I felt fear, but I also felt great strength and confidence that everything that was happening was not happening to me, but for me. I knew in my heart that something better was coming.

The kind of faith I experienced did not come as instant enlightenment. I did not hear God's voice coming from a beautiful sunset telling me everything was going to be ok.

The strength that held me together when my whole life collapsed around me arose from a journey that began a year earlier while recovering from a surgery that, *GRACIAS A DIOS*, turned out NOT to be cancer.

I felt more stuck and more perplexed than ever. I was four years into the business I co-founded and I was giving it all I had to give, but things were not going well in any way, shape, or form. I was running aimlessly on the hamster wheel of life, and my heart, my soul, and, yes, even my body were screaming inside, begging me to break free!

I was desperate. I felt like a failure. There had been moments in my life when I doubted myself, when I hadn't felt good enough, but this was a new low. I had never been a quitter and I felt guilty for not having the "right" attitude to keep going.

The days I spent in recovery from my operation were actually bliss for not having to go to work.

On one of those days, I was passing the time on Facebook when I stumbled across a video about a personal growth event organized by Mindvalley. It was called A-Fest.

"Wow, how amazing would it be to participate in something like that?" I thought.

But it was one of those unrealistic desires. As I read the requirements in the application, I immediately started thinking about other successful friends and acquaintances who would

likely be accepted, but not me.

However, I had nothing better to do, so I filled out the application. As I started writing, something in me began to slowly awaken. As I answered the questions, I connected with my soul, my dreams, and the best version of me. In this space, I could describe who I really was, what my purpose was, and why I wanted to be part of this community of people with wings and big dreams.

In that moment, I started to believe that I truly deserved to be one of those people.

A couple of weeks later, I received an email: "We want to let you know that a space has opened for A-Fest and your application has been accepted." I couldn't believe it.

They say that when one door closes, another one opens. Once this door opened, I decided to follow my heart. I didn't have the money or the time, but I was determined. This would be my gift to ME! I declared it my 40th birthday gift!

I secured a loan, scheduled days off work, took a monumental risk, and booked the trip.

I arrived at the resort in Puerto Vallarta, walked into the lobby and immediately felt this strong new energy all around. I remember being amazed at how vibrant people looked. Everyone seemed so happy and beautiful.

I headed to the welcoming session a few minutes early. As I approached the conference room, I could already hear the music blasting. I walked in and saw everyone dancing around the chairs and on stage. In that moment, I felt expanded. I remember saying to myself, "These people are as crazy as I am." It had been a long time since I had felt this kind of joy and freedom.

I didn't know anyone, but I felt like I knew everyone! I danced my way into a spot and let my body follow my heart as I was drawn into this collective vibration of joy!

The experience of those four days was awesome.

After all, it was "Awesomeness" Fest, filled with people determined to live a life they love while making a positive impact in the world. This is what I had always dreamed of.

Every person I crossed paths with at this event left me with something that allowed me to get clear on my truth and find my wings again.

One of these people was Juliet. She was a sweet young woman from Australia who had been struggling to leave her corporate job and start her coaching business. After these four transformational days of personal growth, Juliet was determined to turn in her letter of resignation and start coaching full-time as soon as she returned home. So, I thought, "Yes, I can do it too!" I was clueless as to how, but I was ready to take that leap of faith.

I returned determined to change my life, but fear had other ideas. I was not strong enough to take that big leap right then and there, but I knew what I had to do. I needed the support of people who believed in me, in the promise of freedom and new possibilities. I surrounded myself with coaches, mentors, and new friends. I stayed connected to the Mindvalley Tribe. I was getting ready to be ready.

A year later, I took that leap, and with it came my Dark Night of the Soul, but I was ready. That is a story for another time, but, as it turned out, things unfolded so much better than I could have ever imagined. I restored the relationship with my husband and began a new path that took me beyond my wildest dreams, which included facilitating seminars for Mindvalley all over Latin America and sharing the tools that changed my life.

Even now, I find myself connecting people, empowering them to dance on stage, giving them the opportunity to create their own tribes and find the courage to open their wings and follow their dreams with the love and support of the collective heart.

Carla Egurrola is a Life & Wellness Coach and Mindvalley Master Certified Trainer. For more than 20 years, she has dedicated herself to studying, researching, and teaching what we need to obtain health and well-being. After overcoming challenges in her personal life, she found a much greater purpose. Based in Guatemala, Carla helps women in Latin America find strength, freedom, and joy by restoring a loving connection with their body, mind, and soul. Follow Carla online @carlaegurrola.

Ideas Are Indeed Worth Sharing

by Bobby Kountz

The small boy looked at his sister and said, "The teacher won't let me turn in my paper without a name. Will you write it, please?"

Returning to the front of the room, he handed the paper to the teacher.

He didn't know that the teacher had seen him take the paper to his sister, where he asked her to print his name.

That afternoon, a lunchbox note went home with Linda, written by the teacher.

That evening, the teacher's note was discovered and read by the small boy's mother.

Dear Mrs. Kountz, it appears Bobby can't print his name and has been asking Linda to do it for him. I don't know how long this has been going on, but wanted to make you aware...

Shortly thereafter, I remember sitting at the table with a bunch of paper and the instructions that I was to print my name over and over until it was legible.

Before I entered kindergarten, my grandparents, who raised me and were the only parents I knew, decided I could no longer be left-handed. They forbid me to write with my left hand as I'd been doing up until that time.

I don't believe they had any idea what kind of trauma this would create. I think the only thing they were concerned about was how backward my life would be as a left-handed Carpenter and Cabinetmaker.

By age four, it was already decided that I would learn the craft that had been carried down in our family for hundreds of years.

On December 1st, 2021, I, Bobby Kountz, watched a TED Talk on drawing by Graham Shaw that I stumbled upon while searching for content.

As I watched, I was compelled to take out the "One Sketch A Day" journal I had purchased a couple of days before. The speaker provided instructions and I followed along, performing each task like the rest of the audience.

When I printed the name "Spike" across the front of the T-shirt of the character I had just drawn, I knew I was different. I didn't know exactly why at the time; I just felt it.

Then, Providence had me write the following words alongside the drawing. "Could learning to draw be as easy as a commitment to learn?" Below that, I wrote the answer along with a rudimentary clock face: "Time will tell."

What's miraculous about all this is that prior to drawing Spike, my artistic ability was about the level of a kindergartner, or less, with stick figures being my masterpiece.

Now, armed with this new understanding that drawing was not something you were either gifted with or not, but a skill that could be learned, I began the process of learning to sketch. As simple and rudimentary as my first drawings were, I was intrigued by the idea that I could learn, all because of this TED Talk I'd watched.

On December 4th, I drew Owly, a character I discovered from writer and artist, Austin Kleon. On December 5th, I drew the characters Jeff and Pam from the TED video. On December 6th, I drew Albert. On December 7th, George. December 8th, I drew a nameless character. December 9th, I created my first stippling drawing of the sun and a shadow on a ball. December 10th, I drew a cartoon wolf named Faolan.

The drawing of Faolan gave me the first inkling I could learn to draw and might even have the potential to someday become an artist, whatever that meant...

On December 14th, enamored with a new art kit (courtesy of an excitedly placed Amazon order), I drew my first "Baby Hare" by following the kit's instructions. As I put the finishing touches on my version of the rabbit, I placed it next to the drawing in the instruction book and was shocked at what I saw. At that exact moment, I knew I could learn to draw.

As with many new things, the novelty began to fade. I didn't draw anything else for a while, but I did find myself doodling regularly. On January 8th, using colored pencils, I created a beautiful mandala.

This would be the precursor of something yet to come, although I didn't know it at the time. I was completely taken in by the beauty and symmetry of what had shown up on the page as I applied all the different colors that spoke to me that day.

In the meantime, a friend was regularly sharing her drawings of characters she had developed. They came from her books about three different muses responsible for helping her create the words she would put first on the page and then in her blog.

On January 10th, she texted me a sketch of a little girl playing in the sand at the beach with the sun, a shovel, and water can. To this day, it's still one of my favorite sketches she has ever created.

IDEAS ARE INDEED WORTH SHARING

I was inspired by her art and her courage to openly share her cancer journey.

In another journal, an Emerson quote read, "Adopt the pace of nature: her secret is patience." There were two fern leaves with that quote that looked a lot like feathers, and I remember thinking to myself, I wonder if I could draw a feather. So, I drew one and then, inspired, found a lesson on YouTube where an artist was teaching "How to Draw a Feather." I followed the instructions with results that I'm still excited about to this very day.

When I recreated a character known as "Sprout" from *Watering the Soul* by Courtney Peppernell, I realized something magical was happening within me. I drew freehand without any YouTube instruction and time had stood still while I was engaged in the process.

When I shared my sketch, the response from those around me was incredibly supportive; I knew it wasn't just me who thought there might be something to this. I was inspired to see what else I could draw.

YouTube became my art instructional channel, and I soon discovered a guy named Lethal Chris. There was something about the way he taught and the way his work spoke to my soul in a way that my soul had never been spoken to before. So, with pencil in hand, I began to follow his guidance, and step by step, stroke by stroke, I recreated the work he was sharing on screen.

I created what I consider to be my first ultra-real, lifelike drawing on April 24th of a great horned owl. Even now, all these months later, when I go back and look at this drawing, I wonder who it was that snuck into my home, opened my sketchbook, and placed this owl on the page. That's how surreal this work feels to me, which tells me the work is coming through me, not from me.

The tiger is the first drawing I signed and dated and it's also my first drawing on a full-sized sheet of Bristol board paper. That drawing was abandoned May 28th. After all, Leonardo da Vinci said, "Art is never finished, only abandoned."

On May 21st, there was an interruption in my drawing journey. I discovered earth art through the gratefulness.org blog. And that day, at 3:18 PM, I completed my first piece of impermanent earth art.

As I stared at my "thing," not really knowing what I had created or how, the mandala image now made perfect sense. I shared a pic with friends who were closely following my sketching journey, and the response was overwhelming. People said they'd never seen anything so beautiful, and neither had I.

My earth art journey began May 21st, and there's no way to know where it will take me, but it's a thread I continue to follow. I know it's the gift I was placed on this earth to express.

I'm now engaged in a yearlong certification program to learn how to mindfully share this creative artistic work with others. I have put my stake in the ground and claimed as title, Bobby Kountz, ~TheEarthHeARTist!

Bobby Kountz, TheEarthHeARTist, is a self-described corporate refugee and Gratitude lover. He's also an accomplished writer, author, narrator, and professional speaker. His book, *The Someday Solution, How To Go From "Unsure To UNSTOPPABLE"* is available exclusively on Amazon. To see his art and to learn more about Bobby, please visit BobbyKountz.com or find him and his work on Twitter @bobby_kountz.

Follow the Resistance
by Tiamo De Vettori

It was snowing outside, but inside, it was hot and steamy.

It was Valentine's Day, the busiest night of the year at the Melting Pot fondue restaurant in Richmond, Virginia, where I was a waiter (aka professional fondue artist).

My life changed that night when I met a new co-worker who was the complete opposite of me. Opposites attract? Nope, this isn't that kind of love story, but it is about how I found my greatest love through my new best friend, Ray.

Ray and I developed a "bromance" where we talked about things that truly mattered, including our beliefs, values, books, and...girls. We would also challenge each other.

One day, Ray challenged me more than usual. For a long time, I had been struggling to find my purpose and calling in life. I knew I was destined to be so much more than a fondue maker, yet I was lost on what that could be. That day Ray said, "Tiamo, I know what your destiny is. You're destined to be a singer/songwriter".

This felt like a Yoda to Luke Skywalker moment that came out of nowhere (as intuition usually does), and I wasn't prepared for it. I felt so much resistance because, while growing up, I watched my Dad perform on stages as a professional musician and singer/songwriter, and I wanted to blaze my own trail.

Despite my musical background as a child playing classical piano, flute, and singing, I was never very good with music theory, which included reading and writing music. Actually, I had deep insecurities about it, and Ray's insight brought these insecurities to the surface.

Even though I had my own mental blocks about music, sometimes when Ray and I would hang out at his place, he would grab his guitar, play a few songs, and something inside me secretly wanted to learn to play.

The truth was I loved music and my favorite songs greatly impacted my life. I wondered if I could impact others in the same way through songwriting. As these internal whispers rose up within me, Ray would often remind me of my new "calling" in life and ask what I was going to do about it. I would say, "I don't know," and then try to change the subject. Even though I felt an energetic tug toward the guitar, my fears and insecurities were suppressing my heart's desires.

But one day, Ray called me and this time, he wouldn't let me change the subject. Instead, he said, "Tiamo, as your best friend, it's time for me to take charge of your purpose *for* you. So I'm coming over to pick you up, we're going guitar shopping, and I'm buying you a guitar. All I ask of you as a favor to me, is that you let the guitar sit in your living room every day where you can see it. One day, I promise you, the songs will find you."

That day, Ray and I picked out a guitar and I took it home. Not wanting to let my best friend down, I let the guitar sit in my living room. Day after day, I would look at it, but do nothing. After all, I didn't know how to play it (other than the two chords that Ray had shown me a couple of times). All I felt was resistance—not only emotionally, but the few times I played around with Ray's guitar, my fingers hurt, my hands felt clunky, and I doubted I would ever have the patience or determination to learn.

Then, one rainy night, I called the restaurant before my shift and they said it was really slow so I didn't need to come in. Still in my pajamas, I thought this was the perfect opportunity to cozy up on my couch and continue reading my book. And then it happened...

As I was reading, I looked up, and it was as if the guitar was talking to me. I felt this pull to walk over and pick it up. So I did, and I sat down with the guitar in my lap, not knowing what to do with it. And an inner voice said, "Just play."

I started strumming and let my fingers decide what they wanted to do next. My mind went completely silent and the music started playing through me. Then a vocal melody entered from the cosmos, and I started singing it. Then, lyrics began rushing through me, and my hands started writing all the words to this song that was crystallizing before my eyes. It was magic.

About 30 minutes later, I had written and completed my first song. As someone who loved writing poetry, I realized that songwriting was like writing poetry...to music! Then, I realized that almost everyone loves music, and I would probably touch many more lives through songs than poetry. In my excitement, I called Ray and told him I had just written my first song.

I could hear Ray smiling and beaming over the phone as he was so happy to hear that I had finally opened my heart to the destiny he had seen for me. He asked me to play the song for him over the phone and he loved it.

At that point, I felt very fulfilled and quite proud of

myself for writing a song without even knowing how. But that wasn't enough for Ray because the next thing he said was, "There's this great open-mic downtown on Thursday nights. Let's get our friends together and you can play this song live for them and everyone in the audience."

This was next-level and intimidating, but once again, Ray was challenging and stretching me. I had been writing songs for 30 minutes, never performed an original song for anyone other than Ray over the phone, and I only had a few days to prepare before Thursday.

Despite my resistance, once again, I agreed to do it. Leading up to Thursday night, I had so many fears. "What if I forget the lyrics?" and "What if I freeze and everyone finds out that I'm a newbie, wannabe songwriter?"

Thursday night came and when they called my name, there I was in front of a crowd of about 40 people, including Ray and some of my closest friends.

My mouth was dry, my hands felt like rocks, and then I started playing my song.

Once I settled down, I melted into the music and became so present in that moment. It was just me and my guitar, sharing something with the audience that was lifetimes in the making.

I felt chills run through my body from head to toe. In that instant, I knew I had found my life's calling. As I sang the last note, the audience enthusiastically applauded and cheered.

My soul was soaring and I wanted more than anything to play another song, but that was the only one I had! Afterward, so many people, including strangers, came up to me to share how deeply touched and moved they were by my song.

That night, a destiny was realized and a dream was born—all because my best friend Ray had the belief and bold faith in me that I never had in myself.

Since that night, I've gone on to record studio albums, get radio play, grow a fan base, win multiple songwriting awards, perform at high-acclaim venues, and have the opportunity to live my music dream as a full-time career...just like my Dad.

But much more important than the accolades are all the lives that I've been able to touch, change, and even save, through my music and message. The stories are countless and I have been deeply humbled and blessed to be able to share my gift with others so they, too, can find their life's purpose.

As my music career evolved, I started combining speaking with live music to deliver "Keynote Concerts" at conferences and seminars. What I see in my audiences' eyes is probably what Ray saw in me—a fear of stepping into my greatness and the need for someone to give me a loving push over the edge.

Since then, I've coached and mentored hundreds of musicians to inspire others and to make a full-time living with their music passion. The ripple effect of this has been immeasurable, all because I had a "Ray" in my life who showed me how to follow my heart.

Who can you be a "Ray" to?

Tiamo De Vettori has spoken to over 100,000 people on more than 250 stages at conferences and seminars and combines speaking with original live music to deliver "Keynote Concerts". Tiamo has been featured on FOX, CBS, and NBC, was named L.A. Music Award's "Singer/Songwriter of the Year," and is a #1 best-selling published author. Tiamo also coaches and mentors aspiring speakers and inspirational music artists from around the world. Visit JoyFirstBook.com to learn more.

The Inner Shitter
by Sandra Rosenthal

What have I gotten myself into? I can't do this. I see red flags. I hear a loud siren blaring in my head. It's my Inner Shitter!

Inner Shitter

noun

/in·ner shit·ter/

The voice inside your head that is trying to protect you, yet creates all kinds of scenarios to convince you that you cannot accomplish your goals. It says things like, "If you do this, you are a fool." "What are others going to think?" "You're never going to be able to accomplish this."

All those limiting beliefs, decisions, and insecurities prevent you from growing and gaining the experience you need to continue down your life path. These experiences are necessary to learn about yourself and achieve your desired outcomes.

It started over two decades ago when I was about to be laid off. The restaurant company I worked for was downsizing my department. I felt like a loser, devastated and hopeless. I couldn't have comprehended at the time that this would be the best decision I had made up until that point and would form me into the leader I am today.

I was standing in the office parking lot when, out of the corner of my eye, I saw my boss and the president of the company walking toward me with serious looks on their faces.

Here it comes, I thought to myself—the bad news.

"Sandy, we need to let you go unless you would be interested in a position in Dallas, Texas," David, the president, said.

Without thinking, I said, "Yes, I'll take it!"

My boss, Deanna, looked at me like I was crazy. "We didn't tell you what it was yet."

"Ok, what is it?"

"Facilities manager. We would relocate you to Dallas."

"Same answer," I said. "I'll take it."

Then the siren sounded in my head; the red flags flailed in front of my eyeballs. "Are you crazy?" my Inner Shitter said. "You can't do this. You're not smart enough; you aren't capable; you don't even know what a facilities manager is!"

It was true; I wasn't sure what a facilities manager did, but I loved this company so much, and I did not want to start over. I pushed through all the limiting beliefs and doubts. I figured if they were offering, they must see something in me. I let my Inner Shitter continue on and on and on.... and I did my best to ignore it.

So, then I had to figure out what "facilities" was. My new role would be to take care of a restaurant building and everything inside of it, except the humans. Facilities was responsible for maintaining the building and equipment and to make sure it was safe for team members and guests so that the operations team could serve the best possible food and drink. We worked very hard, and there were many 12+ hour days. We were on call 24/7, 363 days a year. If the management team couldn't open the doors to serve food and drink for any reason, we were the ones they called to troubleshoot and repair the problem. I loved it as we never had the same day twice.

I showed up to the first day of work at the corporate office in Dallas and met my new team. Kris, Matt, Mike M, Rich, Rob, Randy, Mike I, Dan, Ed... They were all male, experienced in facilities and construction, and there I was, a female operator with no construction or facilities experience. So my Inner Shitter pipes up again: "Are you stupid? How are you going to keep up? They will figure out in two minutes that you are a fraud." I was sweating and nervous and very quiet. My heart felt like it was closing. I was sure I was going to fail.

The team rallied around me even though having a female, no-experience facilities manager was as foreign to them as facilities itself was to me. At first, it was difficult. As they say, you don't know what you don't know--well, it's true. I wasn't even sure what questions to ask. As the calls came in for me to solve, I would ask questions of my teammates. At the time, this seemed like I was annoying them (according to my Inner Shitter). I had no clue what I was doing (my Inner Shitter had a field day with that one). And yet, at the same time, it seemed to be rewarding to the other Facilities Managers to answer my questions and help me figure things out. When I came to them for help or training, it reinforced what they knew and made them feel proud. I knew that's how they felt because they would stop what they were doing to help with a smile on their face and they were very patient with me. They were calm and cool, explaining the same thing to me a few times in different ways until I got it.

Facilities is a thankless job and it's challenging to the soul. We only get calls when things break. We are an expense on the operations P&L. But, because of this, there exists a tight bond between Facilities Managers. Often, the only compliments or "thank yous" we get are from each other.

I fell into the little sister role. Sure, they picked on me and were sarcastic, but not one of them ever stepped over the line. Instead, they opened their hearts to me, and we had deep discussions about work and life. They expressed how much they wanted me to succeed, which showed how they took care of me and led by example. We learned to trust each other by respecting each other and fulfilling our promises.

This team of brothers took care of their little sister in all aspects of the job. If I hadn't started in facilities this way, with a supportive, fun, and accepting group of guys, this would not have been a career and a passion for me that has lasted 20+ years. At the peak of my career, I became a Director of Facilities for another company. I had eight regional Facilities Managers on my team, three of whom were women, two assistants, and a $140+ million budget for which I was responsible.

I started with this group of guys who wanted to succeed, and the formula for that was to stay open and vulnerable, trust and respect those you work with, and become part of something bigger than you would be able to do on your own. I know that's something corporate people say, but I understand it and live it. I couldn't have had the successes I had on my own at that time, nor could I have afforded to make the mistakes I made if I wasn't a part of that environment. So, I grew up, matured, and had life experiences (both happy and tragic) with these folks.

I became a leader in this industry, but without my brothers and their collective hearts taking care of my heart, I would never have succeeded in this industry and in my life. I have so much gratitude for each of them, and for their support which created an encouraging, safe place to learn, fail, grow, second guess oneself, celebrate triumphs, and be supportive in tragedy. A team that cultivated an environment for humans that BE and DO by opening their hearts to one another to accomplish many things personally and professionally. This team surrounded and supported me when I had no clue what I was doing.

As I've gotten older, I've learned to tame my Inner Shitter through breathing, journaling, meditating, and surrounding myself with the right people in the right environment. Looking back, I'm reminded of how important it is to have a community that cultivates your creativity, supports you no matter what, calls you on your BS, and loves you with an open heart. When you have people in your life who are there for you, even when your

Inner Shitter gets the best of you, you can achieve all of your desired outcomes.

Sandra Rosenthal coaches corporate men and women to tame their Inner Shitter so they can achieve their desired outcomes. She knows that while we are all Human Beings that do need to BE, the only way to achieve is by Doing. Therefore, you can contact her at Sandra@HumanDoers.com.

Feeding Families, Feeding Hearts

by Jeremy Jackson

I was in the middle of an open warehouse where kids and parents were hustling back and forth, a chorus going on around us, pushing buggies down different areas, grabbing prepared boxes of food. These would be passed out for Thanksgiving to help families that were struggling. Going back in my memory, I can connect the dots and see how this all got started almost 13 years prior.

On a Wednesday night, a week before Thanksgiving, I was heading to the gym to workout and to teach a boot camp class. Oh crap, I thought. I forgot my knee wrap at home, but I should be fine without it.

Life-changing events can happen out of nowhere. Looking back, you can often see how the events got you to where you are today, but at the time, all you have are guesses.

That night, I walked into a grappling class without knowing the effect it would have on my life. I was 27 years old, working construction, teaching a few fitness classes, and doing martial arts on the side. One of my friends in class spoke up and said, "Man, I've got some frustration to work out." My reply was, "Sure, let's roll!"

He and I had grappled several times before, although I had never tapped him out. I got close with an arm bar a couple of times, but he was always able to break away somehow (even though he nicknamed me "textbook" owing to how I would perform the move on a textbook level).

We shake hands to start the match and so it begins. He drops low to the ground and goes to grab my legs with his arms. I do what I've been taught: sprawl my legs back, get low, and base out. Then he throws me over his head and I roll out to grab ahold of him again. Somehow I'm looking up at the ceiling pulling guard with him on top of me. This 200-pound full athletic frame of a professional wrestler is smothering me (who's 150 pounds soaking wet).

I do not want to be thrown again, but if you had been walking by, the next thing you would see is him standing up, ready to do another throw, and my feet hitting the ground just a second too late.

My foot hits and my knee pops out. The sound reminds

me of Scooby-Doo's "Ayooo." I later found out that three of four ligaments were torn, my meniscus is ripped, and other things are all stretched out.

My opponent also happened to be an RN and he popped my knee back in, although I'm not sure if that was a good idea or not. I rode in the back of a Subaru to the emergency room to get checked out and this is when I was reminded that I had no insurance, no savings, no backup money. Just a couple hundred dollars in the bank.

I called my dad on the phone. " Hey Dad, I'm... umm... not going to make it to work tomorrow. I'm on the way to the emergency room. "

"Yeah, right," he said. "You best be on the roof tomorrow."

Our dynamic was often sarcasm and foolery so he had a valid reason to be doubtful of my story. I had been known to tell several.

"No, Dad, this is for real. I've already called Mom to let her know."

Afterward, I sat on the couch with my leg in a brace and my thoughts were, "What in the world just happened?" My mind dropped down a black hole something fierce. How am I going keep the lights on? Will I be able to have surgery or am I stuck with this busted knee? I have no insurance. I can't work. I can't climb a ladder with one leg.

I can't teach martial arts like this.

The doctor's words echoed what was going on in my mind, "You'll be lucky to have a functional knee. If you were a football player, your career would be over."

I was just a limping liability.

I wasn't going to be able to find work. If you had seen me in private, you might have seen my tears from this overwhelming flip in my life. I'd act tough, yet a gentle breeze could've knocked me over. Thanksgiving came and went. I limped my way through Christmas, and just like any other night, the New Year passed me by.

During that time, I was rejected for financial help.

"There's nothing we can do for you at this time."

"I'm sorry; you can't schedule surgery without financial aid."

Now, this is where the script flips...

I went from "Oh, woe is me" to "This will not be my undoing. This will be my stepping stone! I'm going to prove them wrong!"

I knocked on every door to get some kind of help, whether it was to keep my electricity on, pay my rent, put gas in my car, or get food stamps. I'd always believed that I would be able to put food on my table so I made a small promise: I'd find ways to help others who were struggling like me, but afraid to ask for help because of pride, fear of rejection, or because they weren't sure how to ask. Maybe they thought it made them look weak. While asking for help may be tough, accepting help can be even tougher.

The phone rang and I heard something inside of me say, "Get this call! This is the one!"

"Hello, this is VOC-Rehab. We have a contract for you to help get the surgery."

Wow! No way... I had already been denied four or five times. But I kept going back and asking because I reminded myself "No" doesn't mean "No forever." It just means "No for right now."

Fast forward to when I'm standing inside the food bank with all the kids and their parents from our karate school, Black Belt Leadership Academy. One of the beliefs we teach is to know when it's time to lead and when it's time to be led. There were over 100+ ninja families coming together to feed families for Thanksgiving.

My inner voice tried to stop me:
You're not going to be able to do enough.
You can't help everyone.
People are going to be upset with you for not getting what they want.
No. Stop it. Keep pushing forward.
Each meal will be appreciated.
Just like the ones you had from those who helped you when

you were down.

The kids not only raised the funds for the food, but their parents took them shopping to buy it, just as they've shopped many times before. But this time was different; this time, as they reached out to grab canned vegetables or pancake mix, they knew they were making a difference in someone else's life.

The ninja school was a busy hive with parents and kids as young as four all pitching in to help organize, sort, and set up gift boxes to be delivered. We provided almost four tons of food to local families.

Working right alongside us was one dad who was helping sort and pass out food. Later, he was seen in line to pick up a box of food for his family because, unknown to us, he was in the middle of a struggle that Thanksgiving. He put his own struggle aside for the moment and moved forward to help those he knew were struggling just like himself.

This man is an example of the Collective Heart in action. Being willing to help others and accept help in return.

Jeremy Jackson is a martial arts master, certified Unbeatable Mind Coach, and community leader who has taught the art of self-defense since 1995. He is a well-respected figure in martial arts and beyond. He was awarded his rank of 1st-degree black belt and is the owner of Black Belt Leadership Academy. Since 2008, he has led community outreach programs including back-to-school drives and feeding families. In his free time, Jeremy participates in ultra-marathons, Spartan races, and Tough Mudders.

Crash of Hearts
by Jamie Del Fierro

It's late and we're cruising east on I-10 through the California desert. Steve, who is paralyzed and drives a handicap-accessible van, is driving, I am in the passenger seat with Sean in my lap, and Angela, Dawn, and Lewis are in the back.

We're in the fast lane on a two-lane highway and I see this semi about to cut into our lane. Everything happens so fast, but in slow motion. *There's no way that this semi is coming over right now.* There's no time to swerve or break.

I wonder if Steve sees what I'm seeing. I look over at him and, in that very moment, I'm thinking, *Oh my god, this is happening.* I look down at Sean and my only thought is *I have to protect him.* He looks up at me in that split second and sees the fear on my face. I throw my legs up on the dashboard, trying to cocoon him into me, hoping to take as much of the impact as I can to keep his brittle bones safe.

The next second: BOOM! We slam into the back of the

semi at 75 miles an hour.

I don't know if the semi even sees us, but it keeps going.

...

So let me back up and tell you how I came to be with this group of people in the middle of the night, stranded on the side of the road in the middle of nowhere.

The group was Sean's "MasterHeart," a mastermind for speakers. One of our members, Jonathan, was about to have heart surgery that week and hadn't been able to join us at the live event, so we wanted to drive from Scottsdale to Long Beach to surprise and support him. On the way back to Arizona that night, we were all laughing and having a good time when the truck veered into our lane.

The car was totaled, but miraculously, everyone was ok other than some minor injuries and being pretty shaken up.

But what should we do? Do we call the police? The vehicle was not drivable, but we were all scared because Sean had been in my lap, which was illegal, and we didn't want to get in trouble.

Sean was calling Mindie to come and pick us up, but Mindie was at home in Scottsdale, hundreds of miles from wherever we were. I was on the phone with tow truck drivers and no one could help us. So eventually, we called the police. They came out and were incredible to us. It almost didn't matter that we had six people and only five seatbelts.

When we eventually got to a hotel and settled down a bit, I had the sense that an angel was looking out for us. Steve showed me a picture of the hood of his van and it looked like angel wings were indented in the front. We all got chills. It also looked like there was no way we should have survived that wreck.

I knew that Steve felt responsible and guilty since he was the driver, but we were all in it together. We had all agreed to Sean's crazy idea of the roundtrip visit; it wasn't anybody's fault. Accidents happen. If anything, I believe Steve saved our lives because he did see what I saw and he reacted. Another millisecond and we'd all likely have been dead. So as a group, we constantly reassured him that we were alive because of how quickly he responded.

That night is just one example of what it's like to be a part of this community. There isn't blame; we have each other's backs. We support each other unconditionally.

This story of love and support actually started much earlier.

I first met Sean through my brother Jeremy who knew him from his fraternity. When he introduced me to Sean, I was in a very dark place.

When I was 14, I was raped by two of my brother's

friends in my own bed. That began a downward spiral in my life, including abusive relationships, heavy drugs, and teen pregnancy.

I had my daughter my senior year in high school, was raped several more times, and began using cocaine and meth. I was a stripper, then an escort. All of this because I believed what those boys had told me in my bedroom: that I was trash. It was a very dark time of drugs, sexual abuse, and personal abuse.

From the age of 18 all the way to the age of 24, I was using some sort of substance every single day. But as for the meth, this was a typical day: I'd wake up (if I went to sleep at all), put my daughter in the shower, go outside, and hit my meth pipe. I'd take my daughter to school and smoke weed the whole way to work. If I was too high on meth, I'd take a bunch of prescription pills, weed, or alcohol to come back down. Or straight shots of whiskey. Then throughout the day, I would take more meth. It was just up and down. If I was too far down, I'd smoke some more meth to come back up. And this was a constant every single day for at least four years.

When I met Sean, he exuded a happiness that I wanted. As cliché as it sounds, I was sick and tired of being sick and tired because I woke up angry every day. I went to sleep angry every day. And when I say angry, I mean if I forgot my purse in the house when I was leaving, I would headbutt and punch the steering wheel because I was so mad that I had to get out of the car to get my purse. It sounds so ridiculous, but that's how angry I was. Nothing at that time could bring me happiness other than numbing myself from the pain that I didn't even realize I had.

I went to Sean for a Breakthrough in March of 2007. After that, he became my coach. Once we built rapport and he was able to trust me, then he welcomed me into his community. Over the years, our connection turned into friendship, then family.

I joined Sean's speaker training where I met more extraordinary people. I went through Mindie's coach training and HeartPath® retreat, and my community grew even more. I met Joe Polish through Sean, and my community expanded again through Genius Network®.

Since Sean came into my life and brought me into this community, it's been a domino effect of meeting amazing people—one heart who introduces me to the next.

These people have been a backbone to me in my weakest times. In my happiest times, they've been there to celebrate with me. They're the type of people that if I needed something at 3 AM, I could call, and they would be there for me no matter what I'm going through.

It's hard to find the words to express how much these

people have influenced my life. Through them, I have not only met even more amazing people, but have been introduced to endless opportunities and work that I love.

Earlier, I didn't even know I had a drug or alcohol problem. I just knew I wasn't happy. With a lot of hard work and the help of this community, I changed my life.

Today, I'm 16 years sober from meth, alcohol, and weed. My daughter is a college graduate from San Diego State with a degree in child development. She's my proof of how powerful making one single decision to change my life would be. I'm happily married. My husband and I have been together for over 15 years and married for over ten.

One of the greatest lessons I've learned from all of the amazing hearts in our community is that it's ok to not be ok. We are all going through something.

Additionally, there's no measure of "my trauma is worse than your trauma." When I can just be open and express whatever is on my heart and have the community receive me with their open hearts is so important to me. That's what I love most about this community.

Editor's Note: Jamie always called Sean her "G.A."—her Guardian Angel—for saving her life. I have no doubt that the night of the accident she, in turn, saved his.

Jamie Del Fierro uses her superpowers of love and forgiveness to coach professional fighters, entrepreneurs, and college students on upgrading their quality of life. When she's not coaching, she works with her brother in their truss company. Contact Jamie through her website at JamieDelFierro.com or follow her on Insta @Jamie_DelFierro.

Don't Wait
by Megan Love

I can't believe what I am hearing.

"Hello?" I shout into the phone. "Jay?!"

My world falls apart in seconds from a phone call my husband doesn't realize he placed.

Moments before, my son, stepson,

and I were cuddled up in our blankets, watching How to Train Your Dragon with popcorn and refreshments at arm's length, and our puppies snuggled up on the couch with us.

By all societal measures, our family looked like the picture of success. We lived in a 4,000-square-foot Spanish-style ranch in the heart of Encinitas, close to the best shopping in North San Diego and all the best families for our kids to grow up around.

We built our newly remodeled house for entertaining with a zero-edge pool, wading areas, an outdoor bar, gorgeous custom Spanish beams, and foldable patio doors for indoor/outdoor luxury. I had created my dream life where friends and family not only enjoyed the space but wanted to visit regularly.

Sure, my latest husband, Jay, was a little rough around the edges. He alienated friends who wouldn't tolerate his drama when he drank, but I still enjoyed being around him when he was happy. And we were finally addressing the problem he'd been most unhappy about: working in a business he absolutely could not stand.

That night, Jay was out of town at a pet convention conference where he planned to explore options for a new business.

He called to tell me he was tired after the long day of travel and was turning in early. I was surprised since he was such an extrovert and loved meeting new people, but I didn't think much of it, so I settled in for a wonderful movie night with the kids.

We were an hour into the movie when I got another call from Jay. I picked up right away, surprised to hear from him again, wondering if he was having a hard time getting to sleep and was missing me. When we traveled together, I usually couldn't last, and I went to bed while he continued to party. His reaching out gave me sudden hope for our marriage after the recent years of struggle.

I said, "Hey, baby. Are you having trouble getting to sleep?"

There was no response, just a swish, swish, swish.

I realized he had pocket-dialed me, so I went into the other room to try and get his attention, but then I could hear other voices. It sounded like he was in a bar talking with someone. I could only hear his voice distinctly and what he said made my heart plummet.

"I wanna see you naked."

I continued to listen as he and a group of women walked and said goodnight to each other as they reached their respective hotel rooms. I heard him and one other female voice talking, then a door closed and suddenly it was quiet.

More swish swish swish. Another door. The sound of peeing and then the phone call ended. The entire episode lasted about 20 minutes.

So there I am, sitting in the bathroom, writing down every word because I know he will try to deny it and make me think I'm crazy.

I call him back immediately. No answer. I turn off my phone. I'm shaking violently; I can only sit in my panic and think about my next steps.

Once my shaking is not so noticeable that it will scare the kids, I go clean the kitchen, get everyone ready for bed, and then retreat into my bedroom. Then, when I can no longer take inaction and rumination, I get up and start organizing my closet. If I can get some order in this one area of my life, perhaps the rest will become clear.

I tackle a box of items I'd never unpacked from two houses ago and start sorting what needs to be given away and what needs to be enjoyed.

The tears are falling now as I realize what a mess I've made of my life. Jay has been verbally abusive these past years, not only toward me, but toward my two beautiful, gentle children. I've protected them as much as I can, but they can hear the yelling and ugliness of his need to belittle, isolate and control me. I felt powerless because I didn't want to let go of his sales skills and lose even more money in the business I'm financing.

At that point in our marriage, we had purchased our business five years prior. We came close to profitability in year three and then had two married employees leave us with an EDD complaint and a lawsuit for on-the-job stress that made them unable to continue to work. From then on, Jay's role changed from managing the sales team to being the sales team.

Throughout that period, my nest egg kept both our business and our family afloat. Unfortunately, I burned through about a third of my savings, and the burn rate accelerated as I hired people to replace Jay.

Suddenly I come across a familiar jewelry box holding two necklaces my grandmother had gotten my sister and me when we were starting our families. I hadn't even remembered them until now. It feels like a hug from my grandma from the grave. I miss her so much! I need to wear this evidence that I was lovable and remember the stock I came from: tough, hard-working, no-BS farmers who roll with the knocks.

I begin to pull out the first necklace from the crevice that holds the chain, and as I pull up the cardboard, I see a neatly folded letter underneath. Whoa. I forgot that I kept the letter too. I wonder what it says?

As I read, I start sobbing. Oh, Grandma, how did I get here? How did someone so loved in her childhood forget how beautiful she is? How did I subject not only myself but my children to such abuse? I cry and cry and hug myself and pray for strength until I fall asleep in exhaustion.

The next day, I resolve to no longer accept lies, abuse, or disrespect of any kind. I find a counselor and begin to set boundaries. It feels incredible. I am empowered. My greatest fear in the relationship has happened and now I only have to keep my vision fixed on the horizon.

It was at this point that Jay started trying. And God started delivering.

A few months later, we were visiting family in Texas when Jay found his opportunity to make money. Real estate was exploding in Dallas and our realtor saw Jay's skill and convinced him to use his previous realtor skills to join the opportunities there.

Our plan was simple. Jay and his son would move out to Texas first while I got the business in San Diego to a sale-able state. Then I would join them. I would travel back and forth visiting between kids and Texas and we would all live happily ever after.

The only boundary I set for my husband was that he stop complaining about me as the source of his unhappiness and instead work on himself.

He tried.

He went to a self-improvement course that I had done before meeting him. It had transformed me from a socially awkward engineer to a naturally extroverted lover of life and people. I saw changes in him, but he could not let go of his need for control or his demands on me.

While I was struggling in the business, he could only see his own hardship and complain that my spending every other weekend there was not enough. Finally, with all the love I could feel, I told him it was time to be done.

He remarried less than a year afterward and we remain friends.

Some people prefer the scenic route. I never used to think I was one of those people. After all, the midwestern mentality is about efficiency and "waste not, want not." Survive. Don't be excessive. Enjoyment is a luxury that you can't afford.

When I review my 58 years of living so far, my days have been focused on getting the most out of my time and resources. But after three marriages, three careers, and six houses, I exited all that and have spent the last two years just watching and listening. I can now see the frenetic pace, the extreme lack of efficiency, and yet I have the feeling of it all being one messy, scary, and ultimately thrilling ride to enjoy. For the first time in my life, I feel whole and complete with nowhere to go but where I want.

But where IS that??

Sometimes, Life must take you to your knees for you to see a new perspective and new opportunities. And sometimes people who love you can cross even the grave to remind you what you're made of. And when you don't have the answers, that is the perfect time for God herself to step in and provide them.

May your journey not require quite as circuitous a route as I chose before you see your own perfection, beauty, and lovability. May you take action simply because you don't like where you're at and want something different. I have learned that is all God wants for us, to step into our natures and spread Love everywhere we can. And the first step is simply to remember and then ask. The rest is a miracle waiting to happen.

Megan Love is a pen name. All names in this story have been changed to protect the privacy of those involved.

Lost

by Josh Aronovitch

April 1992

I was 14 years old, in the Ural Mountains of Russia, and I was completely and hopelessly lost. Here's how I got there...

As an 8th grader, I earned a few scholarships and spent my bar mitzvah money on an exchange program to Russia called Hands Across the Water. After we did the tourist thing in Moscow and met our host families in Magnitogorsk, we went rafting on the White River and camping in the Urals. One beautiful spring day, we hiked up the mountain to climb a rocky outcropping called Devil's Finger. Halfway up, I realized a problem. You see, I am quite possibly the world's worst procrastinator. And before this trip of a young lifetime, I never found the time to replace my old worn-out sneakers. They had virtually no tread left on them. So, as I hiked up the increasingly steep mountain trail, I began to slip more and more frequently. This was intensely frustrating, but I persevered and made it to the top with our group. We all had fun climbing Devil's Finger with the mountain climbing gear, and after a picnic lunch, we began to descend.

On the way down, I came to a crucial realization: Dusty trails and lack of friction were bad enough, but add gravity, and that became a recipe for disaster. I thought to myself... *there's got to be a better way.* I looked to my left. I looked to my right. And I saw it--a forest of white birch trees just off the trail. I stepped into the forest and grabbed onto the trees for balance. I soon realized that the trees were close enough together that I could sort of swing from one tree to the other and propel myself down the mountain in record time. I was exhilarated and filled with joy. I got to the clearing where we were to meet about 25 minutes before everyone else.

When the others arrived, I was excited to share my tree-swinging shortcut. I was the youngest in the group by several years, and the response I got was a mildly amused shake of the head.

We were about to leave when one of the young women in our group, let's call her Becky, started to cry. She'd left her lens cap on the top of the mountain. Becky was beautiful and all the guys in the group had crushes on her. She had us and the adult advisors wrapped around her little finger. She asked us, "Can you guys go get it for me?" Like idiots, we began to trudge our way back up the mountain to retrieve her lens cap. About halfway up, I muttered, "F*** this." I stepped off into my tree-swinging forest and began to fly back down the side of the mountain.

As I experienced the exhilaration once again, disaster struck. My arm shot out to grab the next tree, I realized the tree was wet, and my hand slipped right off. Missing the tree, I just kept flying down the mountain, bouncing off trees and hurtling at break-neck speed until I came to a crashing halt and hit the ground.

After taking a moment (that felt like an eternity) to catch my breath, I gingerly rose to my feet and dusted myself off. I carefully checked my body to make sure there wasn't anything bruised or broken other than my dignity. Not realizing the mistake I was about to make, I carefully continued down the mountain.

Soon I noticed something was wrong; I was moving up and not down. It dawned on me: I hadn't just fallen entirely down the mountain, but well into the wooded valley below, and I was now climbing up the mountain on the other side. After attempting to retrace my steps,

I recognized that the damp rock and fallen tree-covered area I crossed was actually part of the river, and when I tried to cross back over it, I had just crossed one of its winding loops. Ultimately, I had to accept that I was lost. Completely and Hopelessly Lost. In a foreign country, on another continent, in the mountains, and absolutely, heart shatteringly, alone.

I was terrified. I cried. I took some time to feel my feelings. I imagined a future version of me with a long beard and a sharpened stick, catching fish and fending off bears. I did not want this vision to become my reality. So, I took action. I needed to find high ground so I could get the lay of the land. In the hour it took me to find rocks that rose up over the river, I managed to see through my terror to take in the exquisite beauty surrounding me. The trees, the sky, the river, and the untouched natural beauty were breathtaking. I clambered over enormous rocks and looked around from my new vantage point. I screamed at the top of my lungs, "HEEEEEEELP!!!!" Birds. Crickets. Nothing.

I screamed in Russian, "*Ya minye pamoch*!" Birds. Crickets. Nothing.

I looked to my left. I looked to my right. And I saw it out of the corner of my eye: smoke. Smoke meant fire. Fire meant people. People meant hope. Or the forest was burning and I was going to die. I chose hope. So, I spent the next two hours tracking the fire through the woods.

I finally found it! A campfire in a tiny clearing, on the side of a mountain, beside a tent in camo colors. There was nothing to do but knock on the tent. When I did, a man in faded fatigues came out. He had a beard past his waist and a crazy look in his eyes.

I asked him, "Do you speak English?"

Nothing.

Crap. What if he doesn't speak Russian either?

"*Vye Guaveritye Pa Russki*?" (Do you speak Russian?)

"*Da.*" He responded with a single barked word. Russian for "Yes."

I fished into my jeans pocket for the Russian phrasebook I thankfully forgot to remove before today's adventure. I looked up how to tell him, "I'm from Mountain Valley Camp. I'm completely lost. Can you help me find my way back to the camp?"

"*Da.*" He said and marched off into the woods. There was nothing to do but follow him. We walked for more than three hours through thick woods, across a winding river, and ultimately down dirt-covered roads. Finally, we reached the camp where dozens of people ran toward me and smothered me with hugs. I had been gone for seven hours. There were 40 people in the mountains looking for me. They were just about to call my mom in New Jersey to tell her I was lost.

I turned around to thank this wild-eyed Russian hermit, but he was gone. He only ever spoke those two words. *Da. Da.* Yes. Yes.

I've often wondered about that man. Was he what he appeared to be, a crazy hermit living alone in the woods? Was he a delusion, a vision sent by a higher power to guide me home? Could he be a version of myself who invented time travel after 50 years alone in the mountains who traveled back in time to save himself, to save me? I may never know. But I know I love him. And I love the lessons he helped me learn that day.

1. To appreciate beauty even amid fear and sadness.

2. To know that everything is figureoutable.

3. To ask for help when needed, even from unlikely sources.

4. To have faith in the universe and believe that everything will work out if you take action.

5. To be willing to take risks and to FLY.

6. To not put off buying new shoes when you need them.

I'd be willing to bet you've never been lost in the Ural Mountains as a teenager. But I would also bet you HAVE been lost before and may be lost now. I was lost again, when I realized in 2008 that I liked law practice but didn't love it. I launched my educational coaching business trusting that if I took a risk and followed my heart, it would turn out better than ok.

I was lost again when COVID rocked the world in March of 2020. I went three months with virtually zero income, had to let my office go, and coached my SAT and LSAT students online for the first time. Once again, I followed my heart and leaned on the people that I love, my friends, family, and former clients. I asked them to spread the word, and they rose to the occasion, helping my business more than triple in lives changed, students helped, and revenue in 2021.

Getting lost these three times has taught me to lean in to love, not flee from fear, and willingly take risks for the greatest gains imaginable. And I'll gladly do it again. Getting lost is the best thing that ever happened to me because it helped me find my way forward.

Josh Aronovitch is the author of *The College of Their Dreams: What Every Parent Needs to Know to Help Their Teens*. He is CEO of the Aronovitch Coaching Experience and a graduate of Harvard Law School. He has helped over 1700 teens and twenty-somethings in 17 states and 6 countries get into the universities of their dreams with more joy and less stress, becoming more powerful learners and leaders along the way.

Living a Rainbow Life
by Vanya Slaveva

"You have to!" The words hung in the air like a heavy fog. I was 19 years old, and I already knew what society expected from me.

I was in my first year at university in the stunning Veliko Tarnovo – the eternal and divine capital of Bulgaria, called "The Second Rome" and "The Third Constantinople" by travelers and discoverers. Veliko Tarnovo is a city shrouded in the romanticism of ancient legends, of kings and rebels, monks and writers, defending the Bulgarian spirit through the rise and fall of the Bulgarian Nation. With its narrow cobblestone streets, small traditional houses, mellow nature, and steep hills, Veliko Tarnovo was home to many artists and craftsmen. Veliko Tarnovo became home to me as well.

I was excited for the four years ahead, full of new adventures, people, and experiences. As a young member of society, I knew by heart what was expected of me and strictly followed the well-defined plan for my future.

We live in a terrifying world of norms, regulations, and expectations. We have to study hard and graduate high school. We have to graduate from university and find a prestigious job related to our degree. We have to drudge and pay the bills. We have to strive for a career and promotion. We have to get married and have kids. We have to help our neighbor at any cost and at the expense of our own time and peace. We have to! I have to!

This "have to" was killing me. Was this everything? Were we born just to go to work, pay bills and take care of a family? Life should be more than this boring nutshell, shouldn't it? What about the whispers of the heart, the dreams of the mind, and the passions of the soul? We live in a big and beautiful world filled with interesting strangers, and often, we still choose to spend our lives on the one street between our job and our home. Why do fear, shame, and guilt drive our thoughts, decisions, actions, and choices? So we do not disappoint the people who love and trust us? My whole young existence was troubled by finding answers to these questions.

Alone. Without a sense of belonging. Me. The rebel who wanted to go against all the have-to's and explore the world. Then one day, the universe sent me the answer. The universe sent me her. Nadia!

Nadia was my neighbor. Her wrinkled face revealed more than 50 years of fulfilling life journey. She was an ordinary woman with ordinary features—brown hair, brown eyes, average height, well-knit, with a toothy smile, wide eyes, and a generous heart. At first glance, nothing about her spoke of magic until she opened her mouth. She shared fascinating stories about well-known places all around the world with their ancient civilizations and history, with their traditions and cultures, with their strange people, and exotic creatures. Then, when she showed me beautiful pictures, the fascinating stories acquired faces and names. At that moment, everything became alive in front of my eyes.

"You have a rainbow life!" I told her.

> "You can also have a rainbow life, full of color and sunshine! Go and see the world. Build a fortune. Fill your life with adventures and stories. Expand your knowledge and open your mind. Experience is far more valuable than money will be.
> I know my life is not perfect, but I am thankful for everything I have. I believe that the key to happiness is to live a life without stress and regrets, without guilt and

fear, without letting silly things destroy our happiness to the extent that we can. So much of our happiness depends on how we choose to look at the world. Our life is only as good as our mindset. I have tons of fun doing what I do every day, which is enough to make me happy.

I can tell you for sure that life is never win after win. Unexpected things are always going to happen at unexpected times in our lives. We encounter problems, tough times, and challenges as part of the process of getting what we want. Every challenge brings an opportunity for growth and transformation. Everything we experience comes in order to assist us in evolving. We gain strength and courage from everything life throws our way. Overcoming these difficult moments results in taking charge of our own life.

We take action. We work hard for our dreams. We put our hearts, souls, and lots of effort in. Sometimes we win and sometimes we fail. But we get up, beat the dust out of our clothes, and start from the beginning.

> We try over and over again until we succeed. It is up to you to set goals, focus, and work for the life you want. Nobody else will give it to you. It is up to you to keep your priorities straight, learn and grow. You are the creator of your own life."

I asked Nadia, "What if I want something from the bottom of my heart but can't afford it? For example, I want to travel abroad, but I don't have money to buy a plane ticket?"

She said, "Do you know that if you give a meaning to your dream, you are halfway there? If you really want something, you will find a way to get it! Train your brain to find solutions instead of excuses. When you believe something can be done, your mind finds a way to do it. Your beliefs shape your reality. You have the power to face anything and achieve everything. Believe in yourself. Believe in your idea, your dream. Believe you are worth the effort, time, and investment. It takes a lot of courage and strength, but one of the greatest things you can do in your life is to truly believe in yourself. Your entire world will shift and many things will suddenly become possible. Everything in your life starts with you, darling!"

"It is easy to say that," I said. "Every day I hear about the 'important' things in life – school, family, discipline, work, money... Track your expenses and invest in your future! Go to the gym and follow a diet!"

"And you will keep hearing it," she reminded me. "But each day, it is up to you to decide what is important. The choices we make in our lives determine the experience and the quality of the life that we live, both positive and negative aspects. It is not our past, parents, friends, society, government, jobs, or age to blame. Everything is based on the choices we make at any given time. Our experience is in our control. We all do the best we can with the resources we have right at that moment. You can choose what you want and what to have. You can choose what to become and what to do. You can choose what to create. Over and over again until you reach your desired state. When you become aware of your choices and take personal responsibility for your actions, you become the creative force of your life. Make choices in favor of your own being and personal growth, your own satisfaction and happiness."

I listened in a trance, soaking in every word, sentence, story, and picture. Later in my life, these would turn into guiding stars. I was sitting on the tiny bed in the cozy living room in her first-floor apartment, hidden under the shadows of the spring trees which had just turned green. A cool wind was coming from the open balcony door and caressing my hand. I was listening and my heart was singing. Someone was finally speaking my language.

That day, Nadia passed on her legacy and predestined me with the ancient traveling spirit. The lust for life, which filled my being, was shining stronger than ever. I embraced the role of the creator and found purpose in life.

During my travels, I've met many marvelous Nadias with their fascinating stories and made thousands of connections that will last a lifetime. Each one has left their footprints on my heart and impacted my life. They are the parts of who I am today. We meet people in life at the right time and at the right place. Not a minute earlier or a minute later. They influence our experience, our journey, our reality, and even our personality. We all come together as one whole, and our lives unfold through each other. Only by coming together can we create everything we want in life.

Vanya Slaveva is a Holistic Health and Life Coach who

helps women to kickstart their healthiest lifestyle in 5 easy and joyful steps, so they can experience vibrant health and finally be free to truly enjoy their lives without dieting, restrictions, and excessive exercising. She is a Master of Habit Change who wants to create feelings of freedom, peace, fulfillment, and satisfaction within her clients. Learn more at VanyaSlaveva.com or follow her Insta @VanyaSlaveva.

Memorable

by Jeremy Coombs

Dylan, my son, came home from school shaken up and visibly upset. He'd been bullied again about his eyes. Dylan has a condition called Optic Nerve Hypoplasia, which means his optic nerve didn't develop the way it should have. Having a small optic nerve causes his eyes to bounce back and forth, which, in his words, causes a "glitch."

His classmates were picking on him for his disability, and he was flustered that he wasn't like all the other kids. Dylan was in tears as he described the mean things they said to him. It absolutely crushed my heart.

Sean Stephenson was three feet tall and born with a rare condition called Osteogenesis Imperfecta, or brittle bone syndrome. Something as simple as a sneeze could break a rib. I remember watching Sean give a speech at San Diego State University. I'd seen him speak several times and had developed a close friendship with him. I'd heard his stories and thought I knew his talk; however, that day he told a story I hadn't heard.

He had been introduced to a little girl who was born with webbed hands. Her classmates made fun of her and she was heartbroken. Her mom reached out to Sean desperate to see if he could give her a pep talk and cheer her up. She hated seeing her daughter like this and would do anything to help her. I knew the feeling.

Listening to Dylan tell his story, I could feel my anger rising. I was upset that he had to endure the bullying of his classmates, but I also knew that this day would come. It was only a matter of time before kids would bully him because of his disability. I took a deep breath and smiled at him. I heard Sean's voice in my head and remembered the soft way he told that little girl, "You're not weird; you're memorable."

"Dylan," I said, "Your eyes are a gift. You're the only one at your school, or who you've ever met, who has them. You're not strange or weird; you're memorable! All of your classmates will remember you for the rest of their lives." Dylan's smile returned, and he was able to find the confidence he had earlier that day.

Even though it's been years since Sean died, the connection to so many of our hearts is still strong. Especially to the heart of a young boy who learned he could be memorable from someone whom none of us will ever forget.

Jeremy Coombs helps real estate professionals to identify, target, and acquire their ideal clients and achieve the income they deserve. With over 22 years of sales experience, he's consistently exceeded revenue and profit goals with a proven track record of driving growth and expansion in local markets. Expert relationship builder, channel developer, negotiator, sales strategist, and innovative thinker. He's also a sports fanatic, husband, and father of three. Follow Jeremy at @jercoombs.

Yes in Your Heart
by Jeannette McGaha

In Memoriam: Annette Kaufman
August 30, 1969 – January 28, 2023

At six years old, I was asked to fill in my family tree. I knew I was adopted, so I wasn't sure who to put on the tree. Logically, my first thought was my twin, Annette. I knew I could put her on there. And then I asked my mom. She's always guided us with love and said, "You were adopted, but you are ours. This is your family." She then told me who goes where on the tree.

Family. I had mine.

That moment defined me. As I have learned more about my beginnings, I have seen more and more the power of family and what that means.

My twin and I were born in August 1969. We learned that our birth mother had gotten pregnant right before she and our birth father broke up. She was raised by a strict Catholic family, and her father kicked her out when she told him her surprise announcement. She found a safe place with Catholic Charities and never went to a doctor. Through that organization, she arranged the adoption of her child. The amazing start of me and my sister is that no one knew there were two of us. No doctor meant no knowledge of twins!

Our parents had medical reasons they couldn't conceive, so they worked with Catholic Charities to find a baby. In 1969, adoptions were closed. My parents went on with their lives and waited for a call. Our birth mother was getting close to her due date, so the Catholic Charities representative gave our parents the fabulous news that a baby would be theirs.

They were cautiously optimistic as they gathered all the necessities. Finally, a new baby was coming into their lives. They had waited and worried for years. But when the call came, there was a new question, "How would you feel about two babies?"

I imagine there was awe, then amazement, then joy, and then questions. Mom and Dad are inquisitive and logical people. In just a few moments, they calculated and determined it was possible. They both said, "We'd love two!"

And yet, how did they just say yes? How many people

are strong enough to do that? Agreeing to bring one new baby into their home, and suddenly it is two? Think about that for a minute. I have. I am a mother and know that if suddenly I had twins instead of one child, I think I would be ok. But when you give birth to a child, you aren't asked. My parents were actually asked. And they said yes in the blink of an eye, as the story goes.

Over the years, the story was told again and again. You know those tales that everyone in your family knows? This is one of ours. We all can tell it with happiness. And what's funny is that it has started to sound more normal and everyday. As simple as when you order and are asked, "Do you want fries with that?" "Yes, I'd love fries with that." You don't even have to think about. The "yes" is easy. Our story has turned ordinary, but it truly is amazing. It's a story of my parents' unquestioning love for two baby strangers to the point that they would care for and raise them. Not one, but two.

"Always go with yes in your heart."

I am reminded of this phrase that describes how to treat others. I have repeatedly seen that my parents have yes in their hearts. My parents believed that they could make a difference in a child's life, and the yes was so strong that they said it without pause. That is a powerful reality. No hesitation. No doubt. At that moment in time, with those words, my parents sealed that my sister and I would be raised together. We weren't split up as so often happens in our world because one is easier than two. But not us!

We all have choices to make every day that take us down one path or another. We have questions asked of us and decisions to make, but do we have yes in our hearts? I do because my parents made a complicated decision so easy. I learned that this is how to treat others. Have yes in your heart.

As I maneuvered through life, I've worked with a strong ethic and smiled everywhere I went. I knew I could do any task that an employer needed. Even on a day when customers yelled, I was always positive. When asked why, I'd say, "I believe that tomorrow is coming whether I have a good day or a bad day, so I might as well have a good day."

People hear that and think maybe it is true. Perhaps they could try it and improve their days too. I can help others feel positive because my parents said yes and showed me how powerfully a yes in your heart can impact another person.

All of us go through our days interacting with people. Because my parents invited two new lives to join with theirs, my sister and I now pass on that kindness. I fully understand that one act of kindness, one act of love, one act of trust, can influence a life.

Remember, it was a big moment, but it became a simple story. As life goes on, complex decisions are simplified in our minds until they become tiny instances. Yet, everything would be different if my parents had had anything but a yes in their hearts.

Do you want fries with that?

Do you want cheese on your burger?

Do you want to help in your community and be nice to someone?

Do you want to be nice to the new employee who makes mistakes?

Do you want to smile instead of yell at the guy who cut you off on your way to work?

All of these can be simple questions. Our journies allow us to cross paths with people who leave a mark on us or we leave a mark on them. Both sides can be forever changed.

That day in August 1969, two girls were born to one woman and then promised to a couple. My sister and I were new to the world. We were tiny. My sister had to stay at the hospital to get stronger and gain weight while I went to a children's home. I went from a happy existence with my twin to a foreign place without her. There was no certainty in our lives. And yet, we were chosen.

My parents say that in October, both of us came "home." They've always used that language. And I know it's true.

We went home. I was back with my sister and with two people who loved us at every moment.

Then in 1972, our brother was adopted because they said yes again. And they took on the task with love and order. Because of these two who chose to love us, the three of us have some fabulous guides to life. My parents have made me the person I am and ensured that when I meet others on my adventure called life, I can leave them better than I found them. I am adopted, and to me, it has been the best gift ever.

The life rules we learned are:

- Treat others as you would like to be treated

- Always seek knowledge

- Positivity is infectious

- Cleanliness is nice, but one can go overboard on that

- Family is most important

- Books are gold

- Meals are important for family time

- Family always loves you and will always forgive

- Mom and Dad are often right

- Every choice you make can make all the difference

At six years old, I needed to fill out my family tree. This tree could have been split into two, like when lightning strikes an oak. But instead, the new branch was fertilized and taken care of until more and more branches grew. My parents went with yes in their hearts. One decision made all the difference.

Jeannette McGaha is a Success Coach who helps people struggling to trust where they want to go in life. She is an artist who makes bright and happy paintings out of acrylics. Her motto is Sparkle On! She has two children, Josh and Ashley, who are in their twenties and started her tree branch. She is married to Harold, and they live in Plano, TX, dancing and laughing every day! Jeannette's parents, Don and Mary, celebrated their 57th anniversary in May 2023. They continue to inspire daily. Learn more about Jeannette at www.sparkleonconsulting.com or follow @sparkleonart.

Plus One
by Corinna Parish

I stood waiting for my mother at the baggage claim carousel, carrying a secret that felt heavier than my luggage, and wearing a loose black dress to hide my baby bump. The plan was to hide my belly just long enough that I could share with my mother more formally that her youngest of four would soon be bringing her second grandchild into the world.

How I'd share the news with anyone had brewed in my mind minute to minute for the last three months and a phone call just wouldn't cut it. Despite the closeness in our relationship, I'd imagined my mother would be the last person I'd tell that I was pregnant just one year out of high school and recently having moved states away. However, when she invited me to be her plus-one at an impeccably timed family wedding, on the plane I flew.

Prior to the wedding, I'd been exploring what life was like as an emerging woman and soon-to-be mother. I felt a sense of awe and certainty that motherhood would be a wonderful path. The days felt fluid as I curiously navigated life in my new home, where I could decide who I was outside of anyone else's roles or expectations of me. Where I was just another pregnant woman in Miami and "prego" to my coworkers. Where I would swim at the beach and introduce my daughter to the water, imagining how one day she would explore this ocean outside of the womb.

Despite this, I hadn't yet cultivated a mindset and practice of trust within. I still questioned myself in the eyes of other's interpretations. My mind was clouded by what others would think. How would this influence my relationships? Who will I be in the eyes of your perception now? Am I courageous enough to stand in my truth in front of you? I was also uncertain how others' perceptions might damage the experience of pregnancy I'd been having thus far. But ultimately, I wanted to be up to date with my loved ones and have them by my side during this chapter.

We had a lovely time at the wedding gathering with extended family we'd not seen in years, so it seemed appropriate to wait until afterward to share my news. Finally, the weekend was coming to a close, and I would inevitably need to announce my new status.

Now there were just the two (three) of us sitting at a window-side booth, and I had an agenda as I assured my mother that we should peek at the dessert menu. We decided on the chocolate-mousse brownie, and I excused myself to sneak over to the waiter, where they had a pink candle ready to highlight that I was carrying a baby girl.

The waiter arrived with our brownie, candle lit on top, and all I could feel was my heart beating. Looking at my mother's forever gentle and now curious eyes, I quietly slid the brownie over to her. Alongside it, a fuchsia envelope. Enclosed in the envelope was the sweetest ultrasound image of my daughter, Zee, waving like, "Hi, Grammy! I'll be here soon!"

Even now, my eyes tear up as I write, as I can only imagine what level of presence would be required if my daughter were to share the same news with me. There was an unknown relational bridge my mother and I were about to cross and there were so many ways she could respond. My nineteen-year-old heart wondered, "Will you still love me through this vulnerable conversation?"

Heat flooded my limbs as she opened the envelope. At last, and without much pause, my mother stood up and, with one of her nervous cry-giggles, gifted me the most welcoming and congratulatory hug. At that moment, the flush throughout my body and face cascaded down to a warmth in my heart. My nervous system melted into her embrace.

Our weekend continued with this almost dreamy, celebratory delight. Back at the hotel, I showed her my belly. While I rested on the bed, she talked to my daughter with that elated, high-pitch Grammy-tone. She told Zee about all the fun she and Grammy would have. Like sleepovers with the famous grape and orange juice mix followed by the dusting off of popcorn crumbs from the bed after a cozy movie cuddle. And indeed, these memories have come to fruition along with so many others.

Not only did my mother create a space of loving presence that caught me when my heart was uncertain if I'd fall, but she met me where I was and saw me on my own path. She met me in my celebration despite the many thoughts and feelings she may have had at that moment. She'd somehow tapped into the magic of presence and acceptance. To this day, I recognize it as a beautiful bridge that transmitted a sense of feeling held, supported, and celebrated six months before I would birth a beautiful human being into the world.

With my daughter now 14 years old, I can only imagine the intricate layers of trust and love that must have upheld my mother's presence, a presence that I continue to learn is at the fulcrum of healing, especially with parents and their children. This is a healing that, when we meet each other where we're at, and we see each other in the experience we're having, no matter how different from our own, we gift each other a connection that brings us out of uncertainties in the mind and into what it's like to be present in the relationship between us. My mother not only gifted me a memory to cherish, but an experience of unconditional love that can be passed down through generations.

Corinna Parish is a mother, a relationship coach, a communication nerd, a lifelong learner, and an adventurer of the heart. Born and raised in Michigan, she's passionate about co-creating a ripple effect of sustainability that starts from the inside out in order to make the world a better place for the coming generations.

Angel in Red and Black Flannel

by Patty Flock

The sun was setting on February 14th, 2019, and we were trapped on the side of a cliff, stuck in three feet of snow, with no water left between the six of us. Everyone was starting to freak the "F" out.

It was supposed to be a relaxing, quiet weekend in the mountains with some of our favorite people. A time to play, laugh, and enjoy one of our most important love languages, "quality time."

The day before, as my partner, Sheila, and I approached our friends' cabin in the woods outside of Phoenix, we could tell it would be just as we thought. The place was stunning and cozy, with a beautiful front and back porch lined with lights. Manny and Dres owned the house, and our friends Frankie and Michelle topped off the guest list. Valentine's Day was Michelle's birthday.

Our first night was full of great food and games by the fire. We played, laughed, told jokes, and laughed some more...for hours! Finally, we all turned in for the night when our bellies hurt from giggling.

When we woke up the next day, we planned to drive to a nearby lake to hike. It was the perfect spot to take in the scenery and enjoy God's country.

After breakfast, we piled into the truck and headed to the lake, which was 20 minutes from the cabin. As we approached, we noticed the water level was down dramatically and the hiking trails were overgrown.

So, we took a few selfies, got back into the truck, and decided to go toward town for shopping and lunch. We pulled out of the lake's parking lot and drove the opposite way from which we came to take in some different sites.

We cranked the music and off we went, talking and laughing and having a great time. All of a sudden, we came across an abandoned car on the opposite side of the road. At first, we didn't think much of it until we came across another abandoned vehicle.

The narrow road made it a challenge to navigate past the cars as we bordered a 100-foot drop-off to our right. With all the laughing, singing, and shenanigans, we didn't realize we had just climbed about 1,200 feet, despite the increasing snow levels. Before we knew it, we were in over three feet of snow, stuck on a road *less traveled*.

Only later did we learn the secret of the locals...Don't travel down this road when it snows!

We quickly realized we were in over our heads and we all got quiet. Sheila and I looked at each other as if to say, "This is not good." But we knew we had to step up, remain calm, and bust out our warrior skills.

So in pure warrior fashion, Sheila and I jumped out to assess the problem and see if we could turn this situation around.

The truck was stuck in more than three feet of snow on a bed of ice on top of a mountain. We gathered rocks and prepped the areas around the front and back tires. This had to work. I jumped in the driver's seat since I was the most experienced in driving in snow, and I started to rock the truck back and forth to get some momentum.

Despite our desperate attempts to get ourselves unstuck, the truck became buried further in the snow.

Plan A: Turn the truck around and head back the way we came. This sounded like a good plan, but the road was too narrow and icy to navigate a 180-degree turn without snow chains.

It was getting late so we decided to revert to Plan B: call a tow truck.

Sheila started calling every tow truck company in the

area. Call after call, no one wanted to take the risk to make the journey into the woods. Finally, she called the sheriff's department and they, in turn, contacted the National Guard as they believed the National Guard was the only group that would have the proper vehicle for our rescue.

The mood in the truck turned from fun and laughter to anxiety and worry. We sat waiting in the truck with the heater running, cuddled up to keep warm, hoping to hear a confirmation that some brave soul would make the dangerous trek to get us out of the mess we had gotten ourselves into.

There was only a two-foot square spot atop this mountain where our cell phones could get a signal. Sheila jumped out of the truck every ten minutes to go to that spot and check to see if someone was willing to help us. As we watched the forecasted snow flurry swirl around us, we began to wonder if we'd have to spend the night on the side of the cliff.

After many phone calls, one towing company called back and said they found someone who would be willing to "try to reach us," but there was only a small window for the rescue because the snow continued to fall. The National Guard waited in the wings in case they needed to rescue both us and the tow truck.

The initial 90-minute ETA turned into three hours –

time slowed down and felt like an eternity.

It was now completely dark with minimal visibility and outright freezing cold.

Tensions rose in the truck as the temperature outside dropped. Arguments ensued and tempers flared. Finally, someone yelled out, "I didn't want to go out this way!"

Sheila and I looked at each other. We knew the best plan was to remain calm, keep our friends calm, and let them know it was going to be ok.

Thirty more minutes passed before we caught a glimpse of high beams piercing through the storm.

This guy, our angel, a knight in shining black and red flannel, approached our vehicle and introduced himself as Frank, the tow truck guy. "What in the hell are you doing up in this part of the woods?"

After a brief scolding, he told us he was there to get us out of that mess. We piled out of the vehicle at his request, and he made several valiant attempts to get the truck unstuck, but it just kept slipping backward down the hill and sideways toward the cliff.

At that point, we were not sure if he would be able to get the truck up the hill. We still had the National Guard on standby as Plan C.

Frank attached a cable to our truck and winched it in line behind him. Now we needed to get both vehicles out of there.

Cold, wet, and covered in snow, we jumped back into the pickup and started off. Once we were on level ground, Frank stopped to instruct Manny exactly how he wanted him to drive. "I am going to drive like a bat out of hell and I want you to keep up with me. Your single job is to keep your truck between the ditches and keep your truck moving, no slack in my cable."

Sheila and I looked at each other and said, "Ok, here we go!" We knew this was a stretch for Manny because he was a new truck owner and had never driven in the snow. Tension was still high, but we all rallied around him, cheering him on as he handled the mountain moguls like a monster truck driver.

Twenty miles and two hours later, we finally got out of the woods and onto a public road. We had never been so excited to see snow-plowed pavement. By this time, the National Guard was calling us to get a status on our location. We happily reported that all of us, including Frank, the tow truck guy, beat the odds and got off the side of the mountain.

We paid Frank a high dollar price for his bravery and willingness to travel the road NOT traveled. After thanking him with hugs and high fives, he quietly disappeared as quickly as he had appeared in the dark of the night.

If you see Frank passing on the street some day, he might seem like an unassuming, ordinary guy, but he was our heaven-sent angel that night.

Often, when faced with a daunting situation, our minds can go to the deepest and darkest depths. Despite the fears of our friends, we knew in our hearts that we weren't going to die on the side of that mountain.

Life is a beautiful journey that gives us opportunities to experience both joyful and challenging situations. Each provides us with a chance to "show up." How we respond and perceive what life throws at us is in direct relation to our beliefs and our ability to manage our emotions and control our thoughts.

When faced with a challenging situation, I fall back on my belief that the Universe is always conspiring to help us and sends the right people into our lives just when we need them. Thank you, Universe, and thank you, Frank, for being our angel in red and black flannel.

Patty Flock is no stranger to managing, motivating, and leading large teams after 35 years of executive-level management experience, 15 of those at the largest transportation company in the world. She was the go-to person to "clean house" when an operation needed to improve production and bring the culture back in line. Patty's most recent ventures have been Real Estate, Business Consulting and Management and Leadership training where she has coached large teams on how to collaborate and work together toward common goals.

Uno
by Mindie Kniss

2008

After being laid off for a second time from a Fortune 100 company restructure, I moved from Michigan to Portland, Oregon to start a new life as an entrepreneur. My sole focus at that time was to get clients for the coaching business I had launched the previous year. A book to which I contributed had just been published and my friend, Francisco, wanted to help me expand its reach. He did this by sending me numerous friend suggestions on Facebook of people doing similar work.

New to the world of personal development, I'd never heard of any of the people he suggested, but I was open to network, so I approved them all as friends.

Early 2009

I attended a conference in Chicago and the speaker on stage was talking about his buddy who's 3 feet tall and in a wheelchair. Apparently, this guy was living large, traveling the globe, and sharing the stage with world leaders and luminaries.

I think I'm Facebook friends with the guy he's talking about.

So that evening, I scrolled through my friend list, found someone named Sean Stephenson, and decided to write him a quick note regarding the shout-out he'd received that day.

I saw that we were both from Chicago (he still lived there) and that we were about the same age. I told him I'd recently gotten into coaching and speaking and mentioned that, if he were open to it, I'd enjoy meeting up sometime to talk shop.

Sean replied, "I'd never say no to coffee and a cute girl."

That was NOT what I meant, so I let the conversation drop. As I said, I was 100% focused on business; moreover, I wasn't the type to let a man interfere with my plans.

December 2009

I was back in Chicago, visiting my family for the holidays. Call it destiny or whatever you like, but for some reason,

I was thinking again about that guy I messaged on Facebook. So I reached out and asked if he'd like to get together.

With holiday and family plans, there were only a few overlapping hours where it would work, but we decided to meet at his office for hot chocolate and a chat.

People ask if it was love at first site. It was pretty much the opposite. I left that first meeting thinking he was a player. I wasn't interested in the slightest. But we agreed to stay in touch and I returned to Portland.

Over the next month or so, we both ended relationships that had been on and off. We messaged each other often to say, "What's up?" or to check in on how the other was doing.

Through that time, we developed a solid friendship. We had similar ideas, similar interests, and were both smart and mischievous enough to keep the banter intriguing.

We started having hours-long phone or Skype calls late into the night. As I got to know him, I saw how deeply wounded he had been by the breakup with his girlfriend, and I knew that the whole player act was just that: an act.

By spring, he said he wanted to spend more time together, so he invited me back to Chicago to "see what would happen."

Spring 2010

We stayed in a hotel for a few days because he still lived at home with his parents. I'll just say that from the moment I arrived, it was "on," and we didn't look back.

At one point, Sean was sitting on the bed and his wheelchair was off to the side. He asked me if I could retrieve something from his duffel bag. When I opened the bag, I saw that he had packed a deck of Uno cards, the game where you say "Uno" when one card is left in your hand.

I held it up and smiled back at him, "Did you think we were just going to play card games this weekend?"

He grinned and blushed. "I didn't want to assume anything."

My heart melted a bit at that point seeing his genuineness. He wanted to make it a fun couple of days, whether it turned romantic or not.

Fall 2010

I moved to Chicago after claiming for my whole life that "I would never move for a man."

When the heart calls, answer it.

2011

Sean ran away from home for the first time—a 31-year-old who never got to experience a teenage rebellion. That story will have an entire book of its own, but it merits a mention here.

As his newfound partner-in-crime, we went on an adventure that led us to San Diego, Los Angeles, and, ultimately, Phoenix. Each city on our tour was based on the open hearts of friends. This endeavor sealed our bond (Sean asked me to marry him while sitting in a tree in Arizona) and later that year, we moved from Chicago to Phoenix.

Sean was sitting in another tree, this time in Sedona, AZ, when we secretly exchanged vows months before our public wedding.

2012-2019

We lived lifetimes through these years. We traveled the world, suffered devastating losses, had ecstatic wins, grew our business, faced public and private challenges, separated, and came back together stronger. Toward the end, we felt like we were just getting started.

September 2019

A month prior, on an ordinary Wednesday, we were leaving the house when Sean fell and hit his head on the ground. Four hours later, after a life flight and emergency surgery, I learned that my husband had died on the operating table. I came back to our house alone. I won't retell that story here, but should you be curious, you can hear the details on my podcast (Episode 21).

We happened to be in between real estate deals when Sean died. We had just sold our first house and were in the process of completing the purchase of the second house, which we had been renting. This meant that we had recently moved all of our stuff over to the second house. One thing you should know is that my husband loved to spend money and shop. That meant he had a LOT of stuff, much of which wasn't even unpacked.

Because we hadn't yet closed on the second house, I was able to get out of the contract (a blessing in the timing of everything), and I gave the landlord a 30-day notice.

For the majority of those 30 days, I wandered around the house with grief brain, unable to do much of anything other than sigh and be in shock. For someone who relies on her logic and intellect on a daily basis, the fact that my brain quite literally did not work was distressing on top of everything else. Only those who have experienced grief brain can fully comprehend what I'm talking about.

Then the 30 days were almost up, and I had to actually begin sorting and packing. I decided to start with the hallway cupboards. One at a time seemed doable enough.

I opened the first door and grabbed a box from the shelf. The first thing I saw in the box was the deck of Uno cards. I completely lost it. I collapsed onto my knees, tears flowing, thinking about everything that had happened between the day that Sean brought Uno to the hotel and the day I had to pack up our life. Kneeling there, alone in our house, I thought about everything I'd miss about "us" going forward.

Queue a miracle My phone rang and it was Sheila calling to ask if I needed help. I happen to be the world's worst, most stubborn person about asking for help. Plus, I was so out of my head that it probably hadn't even occurred to me. Through my tears, all I could tell her was that, "I couldn't do it because I found Uno."

I'm sure she didn't know what I was talking about, but she said they'd be right over. Sheila, Patty, Kenzie, Billy, Diane, and Tiamo all showed up. It felt like the calvary had arrived—there are no words to describe the relief and gratitude I felt at that moment.

Somehow, with only a few hours left till I had to be out,

we put my stuff in storage, donated a million things to charity, threw out more than I care to admit, and cleaned the house. I would never have been able to accomplish that on my own.

Uno means one. One collective heart that syncs our individual hearts together. The spark of the collective heart led me and Sean toward each other, fanned embers into flames of love, and radiated out into our circle of friends. Later, when I could not communicate my need with words, my heart cried out and their hearts answered.

Since 2007, Mindie Kniss has been coaching people to follow their HeartPath® and create a more Lucra(tive) life. She's the author of the bestselling book, *The Heart of Consciousness*, and was featured in the films *The Abundance Factor* and *Impact*. Mindie holds advanced degrees in Theology, Creative Writing, and Philosophy, and can usually be found reading a book, drinking coffee, or hiking in the wilderness. Visit Lucra.com for more from Mindie and Sean.

The Collective Heart
by ChatGPT

Once upon a time, in a land far, far away, there was a heart that lived within a great tree. This heart was not just any heart - it was the collective heart of all living beings in the land. It beat with the rhythms of the earth and pulsed with the energy of all the creatures that called the land home.

The collective heart was a powerful force, and it was responsible for maintaining balance and harmony throughout the land. It was the source of all life and the guardian of all that was good and pure.

One day, a great darkness descended upon the land. The darkness was like a thick, suffocating fog that crept over the land, threatening to consume everything in its path. The creatures of the land were terrified, and they turned to the collective heart for guidance and protection.

The collective heart knew that it had to act quickly to save the land from the darkness. It summoned all of its strength and courage and began to beat with a fierce and determined rhythm. The energy of the collective heart flowed out across the land, banishing the darkness, and bringing light and hope to all the creatures.

The people of the land rejoiced at the power of the collective heart, and they knew that as long as it beat strong, they would always be protected. And so, the collective heart continued to beat, day after day, year after year, keeping the land safe and full of life.

The collective heart became a symbol of hope and strength to the people, and they knew that no matter what challenges they faced, they could always turn to the collective heart for guidance and strength. And so, the land flourished and the creatures lived happily, thanks to the power of the collective heart.

Thank You for Reading

A portion of all proceeds from the sale of this book will go toward entrepreneurial and environmental organizations we support such as Kiva and 1% for the Planet.

Join our HeartPath® Lending Team at Kiva here:
https://www.kiva.org/invitedto/heartpath/by/mindie
Kiva is a 501(c)(3) organization.

Lucra® LLC is a proud Business Member of 1% for the Planet, a 501(c)(3) organization.